Making GIFTS *in* POLYMER CLAY

STACEY MORGAN

NORTH LIGHT BOOKS
CINCINNATI, OHIO
www.nlbooks.com

About the Author

Stacey Morgan is a designer, professional crafter, writer and teacher of polymer clay. At the age of nineteen she started her own business, Tender Heart Originals. She also has a manufactured gift line called NorthStar Critters™ and runs a mail-order business related to polymer clay and her whimsical creations. Stacey is a member of the National Polymer Clay Guild and the Society of Craft Designers (SCD). It is because of her association with SCD and friendship with her mentor Maureen Carlson that this book was made possible.

Making Gifts in Polymer Clay. Copyright © 2001 by Stacey Morgan. Manufactured in China. All rights reserved. No part of this book may be reproduced in any form or by any electronic or mechanical means including information storage and retrieval systems without permission in writing from the publisher, except by a reviewer, who may quote brief passages in a review. Published by North Light Books, an imprint of F&W Publications, Inc., 1507 Dana Avenue, Cincinnati, Ohio, 45207. First edition.

05   04   03   02   01   5   4   3   2   1

Library of Congress Cataloging-in-Publication Data

Morgan, Stacey.
   Making gifts in polymer clay / by Stacey Morgan.
     p.   cm.
   Includes index.
   ISBN 1-58180-104-1 (alk. paper)
   1. Polymer clay craft. I. Title.

TT297 .M68 2001   00-068703
731.4'2--dc21

Editor: Jane Friedman
Designer: Brian Roeth
Layout Artist: Linda Watts
Production Coordinator: Sara Dumford
Photographer: Christine Polomsky

Acknowledgments

To my family, "Yes, the book is now done!" Thank you for your constant support and understanding when I had to work on the book instead of attending some fun family get-togethers. And a very special thanks to my incredible husband who is my inspiration, keeps me going and did all of the typing for this book. I would not have been able to finish this without him. I would like to thank all of my friends and family who gave me constant support and encouragement throughout this entire process: my husband Tim, Mom & Dad (Carol & Ken Mott), Gram (Barbara Searles), the Morgan clan, Annie Lang, Stacie & Karl Peabody, and all of my friends at SCD—you are all so sharing and supportive. I would also like to thank my high school art teacher, Susan Camin, for sparking my interest in sculpting. And to my late Grandma Mott from whom I inherited my sculpting ability. To all

of my customers who return year after year to "see what's new," I appreciate your support and loyalty for all of these years!

There are a great many people that had a hand in the creation of this book. First, I would like to thank Maureen Carlson for sharing her knowledge of polymer clay, friendship and support. This book would not have been possible if she had not introduced me to the wonderful people of SCD (Society of Craft Designers). I would also like to thank Greg Albert for asking me to do this book; my editor, Jane Friedman, for her hard work and patience; and Christine Polomsky for taking all of the beautiful pictures and making the photo shoot go smoothly. I also would like to express my sincere thanks to all of the wonderful and creative people at North Light who made this book come together. My appreciation also goes out to AMACO and Polyform Products for providing the supplies for this book.

Dedication

I dedicate this book to four very special people in my life: my best friend and husband, Timothy Morgan; my parents, Ken & Carol Mott; and Gram, Barbara Searles. I would not be the person that I am or have the confidence to follow my dreams if it were not for these four wonderful people. Gram, you are one of the most understanding, loving and patient people I have ever known and I am very proud to be your granddaughter. Mom and Dad, thank you for always encouraging me to follow my dreams and believe in myself. You have both set a wonderful example of faith, courage and love that will always be a part of me. Timothy, you are my inspiration! Thank you seems too simple to express how much I love and appreciate you and everything you have brought into my life—unconditional love, friendship, teamwork and laughter. Thank you for being the amazing man that you are.

table of contents

Introduction . . . 6

Getting Started . . . 8

Basic Techniques . . . 13

winter

spring

autumn

introduction

I realize that the world isn't always a happy place. However, in the world of my clay characters, I can make it whatever I choose, and you can too! Most of the time I can't help but make a character that smiles back at me. It is my hope that you get as much pleasure from making these characters and learning to design your own as I had in creating them. Polymer clay land is a wonderful place to visit, and before you know it, you will want to go there again and again as you create and grow with your characters.

In this book, besides giving you the instructions for specific projects, I have included a few other ideas that I hope will inspire you to create some of your own designs. I suggest keeping a notebook with you as you read through this book and work on the projects. Then, if you come up with any of your own ideas, or things that you would like to try, you can write them down before you forget.

Getting Started

Let's review some basic information before you begin making the projects in this book.

Polymer Clay

People have different opinions about each kind of clay. Different people like different clay for different reasons. Why not get a small package of each to play with and see which one best suits you? Following are brief descriptions of some polymer clays.

FIMO Classic

Although at times this is the hardest clay to condition, I personally like the results the best. It is great at holding detail while you continue to work on a piece. It is also one of the strongest clays after baking.

FIMO Soft

A softer version of FIMO Classic, it is easy to condition and is available in a range of luscious colors. FIMO Soft and FIMO Classic were used in most of the projects in this book.

SAFETY TIPS
- Wash your hands. (See a special note on page 12.)
- Do not use clay tools for or with food after they have been used with clay.
- Do not eat while working with clay.
- Do not make clay objects that will come in contact with food even after the clay is baked.
- Do not burn the clay.
- Adults should help children and substitute adult tools for age-appropriate tools.

PREMO! Sculpey

This clay is relatively easy to condition, especially if you have a pasta machine. The finished product has a matte finish. I used the PREMO! Sculpey flesh color in all of the projects that required a flesh color.

Sculpey III

This is the clay that most people try first, due to its softness and price. Although I add a small amount of the transparent to my FIMO, I do not recommend its use alone for anything that you want to have around for a while. It breaks very easily.

Cutting Tools

A thin blade is best whether your knife is sharp or dull. Soft clay is easy to cut and generally does not require a sharp blade. If you need to slice a thick piece of clay, such as a cane, without distorting it, a NuBlade works very well.

Glues

Sobo glue

This is a white fabric glue that is a personal favorite of many polymer clay artists. I have found it to be very helpful in attaching clay to porous surfaces, such as wood, paper, cardboard, etc. It also works with some nonporous materials as well. Sobo glue is most commonly applied to the surface and allowed to dry, then the object is covered with clay. The dried glue gives the clay something to attach to. If you were to cover a wooden egg, for example, the surface and the clay would have a tendency to slip around. However, if you cover the wooden egg with glue, let it dry and then cover it with the clay, the dried glue gives the clay a slightly tacky surface to adhere to.

Silicone glue

Silicone glues, such as Goop or E-6000, are great for bonding non-porous materials, such as pin backs, to clay (after the clay has been baked). I do not recommend that children use this kind of adhesive, because of the harsh fumes; adults should use it only in a well-ventilated area. When used properly, it is wonderful for holding pin backs, magnets and button shanks to clay, and it is waterproof.

Superglue

Occasionally I use superglue gel. It can attach raw clay to raw clay, raw clay to baked clay or either of those combinations to porous or non-porous materials. The thing to remember with superglue, other than not to touch it, is that a little goes a long way. So use it sparingly.

MESSAGE TO PARENTS
Although the projects in this book are meant to be enjoyed by everyone, please realize that not all of the tools and materials used are suitable for younger children. I encourage you to work on these projects with your kids and find suitable replacements for adult materials.

Hot glue

I have tried many types of hot glue and have always had the same unfortunate results. They have a strong hold at first, but after a few days or weeks, depending on the brand, whatever was glued together pops right apart. This could, however, work to your advantage if you only want a temporary hold. I would not recommend it for a permanent bond.

Work Surface

If you are working on a surface where you also eat, you should cover the table instead of working directly on the tabletop. This will help keep the clay residue and food away from each other. I personally work on a drafting table, but you can also work on glass, foamcore board, ceramic tiles, countertop or posterboard.

Pasta Machines

Having a pasta machine is not an absolute must, but after using one, you will not know how you ever lived without it. The pasta machine is wonderful for several things:
- creating even, flat sheets of clay in different thicknesses
- conditioning and mixing clay
- rolling clay through with fabric, forcing the clay into the weave of the material
- making a Skinner Blend

And that's just the beginning! If you do not have a pasta machine, the thickness measurements for the different settings are as follows:

#1 = ⅛" (3.2mm)
#2 = ³⁄₃₂" (2.4mm)
#3 = ¹⁄₁₆" (1.6mm)
#4 = ³⁄₆₄" (1.2mm)
#5 = ¹⁄₃₂" (0.8mm)

You can also use a brayer, rolling pin or straight water glass to roll out clay.

BASIC TOOLS

A few basic materials are needed to complete the projects in this book. Any other items needed are listed at the beginning of each project.
- stylus
- dull knife
- NuBlade
- needle tool
- modeling tools
- pasta machine (preferable)
- baking sheet
- aluminum foil
- oven
- blush makeup
- small round brush to apply blush and paint
- blue, black and white acrylic craft paint
- FIMO Gloss Lacquer
- Sobo white glue
- toothpicks
- ruler
- pin backs
- E-6000 silicone glue
- superglue
- wire
- wire cutters

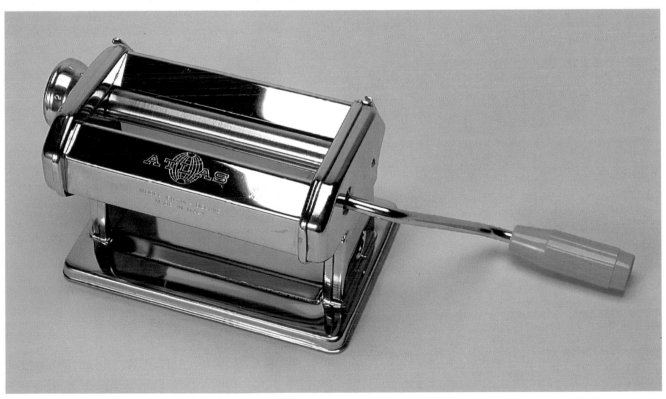

A pasta machine is a great tool (and sometimes a necessity) in polymer clay craft.

Conditioning

All polymer clay needs to be conditioned before you can use it to sculpt. Similar to orange juice after it settles, polymer clay needs to be mixed up before it is good to use. Some clays are more difficult to condition than others, but the end result is worth it. There are a few ways to accomplish this.

• Warm the clay before you start. Put the packaged clay in your pocket or sit on it for a while. You can also warm it by setting it on top of a heating pad on a low setting. When I first started working with polymer clay, I decided to try warming it on a heating pad. It worked great, so I thought I would heat it faster by putting it under the heating pad on

medium heat. About twenty minutes later I returned to find that several blocks of my precious clay had baked under the heating pad! To avoid that kind of heartache, heed my advice and only put the clay on top with a low setting to avoid cooking the clay instead of warming. After the clay is warmed a bit, take it out of the package and cut it into smaller chunks. You can also add FIMO Mix Quick to the clay to help soften it. Begin pinching and rolling the clay. Soon you will be able to roll and twist the clay until you can bend it without it cracking.

• If you are using PREMO! Sculpey clay, you can take semithin slices right off the block and run them through the pasta machine ten

to fifteen times. Once FIMO clay is conditioned halfway, the rest can be finished by doing the same thing.

• If you plan to condition a lot of clay that is a little tougher, such as FIMO Classic, I strongly suggest that you invest in a food processor. Believe me, it makes life so much easier. To use it with the clay you simply need to chop or slice the clay into smaller pieces and put them into the food processor dish. I usually do 8 to 9 ounces (227g to 255g) of clay at a time. Put the lid on and chop the clay for about fifteen seconds. The clay should be chopped up into tiny balls. Press them together in the bowl and then dump the clay onto a sheet of aluminum foil. Finish conditioning by twisting and rolling the clay.

• Here's a little secret. My favorite conditioned clay combination is three parts FIMO Classic (any color) mixed with one part transparent Sculpey III. The Sculpey III does not change the color of the FIMO clay, but it helps the clay to be more manageable after it has been conditioned. You can also use FIMO Mix Quick.

On the left is unconditioned clay; the sample on the right is conditioned.

Clay Gun

One handy tool is a clay gun. The clay gun is a metal tube that comes with several disks. Each disk has a different shape cut through it, and the disks fit into one end of the clay gun. The clay is inserted into the opposite end of the gun. A handle is then attached that pushes or extrudes the clay through the shaped disk. The extracted clay can be used for many things including hair, hay, ropes and strings that need to be a consistent size. In order to save strain on your hands when using the clay gun, make sure that the clay you use is well conditioned, soft and warm. It is not necessary to have a clay gun extruder, like the one seen in the step-by-step photos, but it is definitely a blessing to have. Using a clay gun extruder gives you more leverage without adding any strain on your hands.

Storage

The clay will not air dry, but it is a magnet for dust particles, so it is best to store it in a container. I store all of my conditioned clay in plastic bags. You can also store clay in glass, metal and some kinds of plastic containers. Don't be alarmed if you store clay in plastic and it seems to melt into the container. Certain plastics chemically react with the plasticizers in the clay, and a different container should be used. It is best to store the clay in a cool, dark place. UV rays can begin to cure clay that is exposed. Likewise, storage next to a hot windowpane or heater can affect the clay in the same way.

Measuring

To be honest with you, before I began writing instructions for projects, I never used a ruler to measure the amount of clay that I use. In fact, when I am working on things for my shows or gifts, I pretty much just eye everything. If you need a little more clay here or there, add it and if you have too much, take a little away. After you have worked with the clay for a while, you will not need to measure everything either. However, if you are a beginner, sometimes it helps to use the measurements to get the proportions right.

For the projects in this book, I used the ruler on the cutting and measuring template for polymer clay. If you do not have one or are unable to get one, a plain ruler will do just fine too.

When measuring a ball of clay, lay the ball on top of the ruler. Measure by looking down from the top and seeing which line the very edge of the ball touches. The ball in the photo is a ½" (1.3cm) ball.

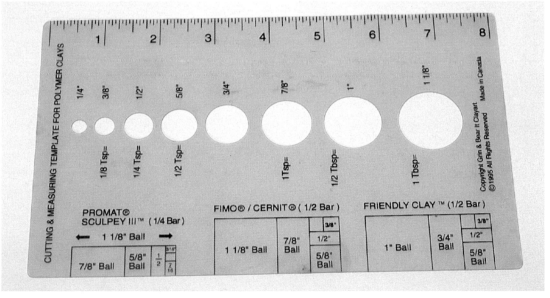

Cutting and measuring template for polymer clay

Baking

Every polymer clay artist has a pre-ferred method of baking the clay. I bake pieces at 250°F (109°C) for 35 minutes. It is wise to test your oven with an oven thermometer. Some ovens run a little hot, in which case you should adjust the setting so the thermometer reads 250°F to 255°F (107°C to 110°C). I prefer to bake pieces at a lower temperature for a longer period of time. This also helps to keep the colors brighter; sometimes at higher temperatures some clays darken a little. Another reason I bake at a lower temperature is to reduce the risk of burning the clay. Severely burning the clay can result in a release of hazardous fumes, in which case you should ventilate the area and leave for a while. Do not confuse hazardous fumes with the fumes from regular baking. The clay does have a very mild scent to it when it is baking. Baking at 250°F to 255°F, I have never burnt a piece (and I have baked a lot of clay!).

I have used a toaster oven only a few times. The particular oven I was using would heat up to 300°F (135°C) and then go down to 250°F (109°C). So if you use one, let it spike first before you put your pieces in. I generally use the oven in my kitchen, and I also have a con-vection oven that works well. Although many polymer clay artists use toaster ovens, I was not com-fortable with the fluctuating temper-atures.

Baking Surfaces

In my opinion the best cookie sheets to bake clay on are the ones manufactured with an air space inside. Line the cookie sheet with aluminum foil with the shiny side down. This helps to reduce the chance of a shiny spot on the bot-tom of the piece. You can also bake with note cards or oven parchment on the cookie sheet. If you bake on something shiny, your piece will have shiny spots left anywhere it touched the shiny surface.

Sealers

Both Polyform Products and FIMO make water-based finishing coats for their clays, and both provide a choice of gloss or matte finish. Some spray glazes are also useful. Krylon acrylic sprays can be used with polymer clay but must be applied very lightly.

WASH YOUR HANDS

Before you work with polymer clay (and after), wash your hands. Although your hands may seem spotless, you wouldn't believe the tiny dust particles and such that end up on the clay if you do not wash your hands directly before working with the clay. Dry them with a paper towel. You can use the paper towel at your work area to wipe off tools when needed. After you are done working with the clay, wash your hands again. If there is clay residue left on your hands, it comes off easily with waterless hand cleaner and a paper towel. Then wash your hands with soap and water.

Basic Techniques

These are the instructions for making the basic head, face, arms, hands, legs and feet used in the projects. Directions for creating a Skinner Blend are included at the end.

HINT
The face can be added either before or after the head is attached to the body. I usually add the face after the head is attached to the body.

Create a Head and Face

Step 1. Start with a clay ball of desired flesh color. The size will depend on the needs of your character.

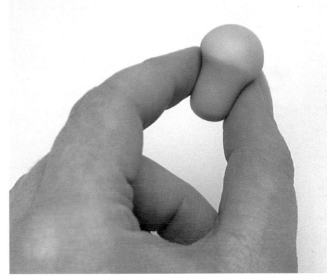

Step 2. Position the ball of clay between your finger and thumb and roll back and forth. The top half should be narrower than the bottom half.

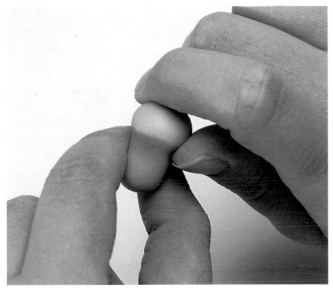

Step 3. With the side of your thumb, slightly flatten the area just above the cheek line.

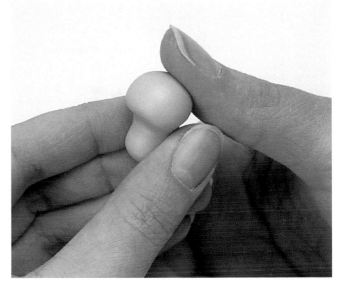

Step 4. With the head still upside down, gently bend the face toward the front just a little.

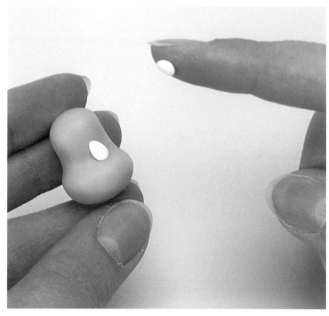

Step 5. Form each eye from a small ball of white clay into a teardrop. Place the eyes side by side just above the cheek area.

Step 6. The nose is a small ball of flesh-colored clay. Place it just below the eyes.

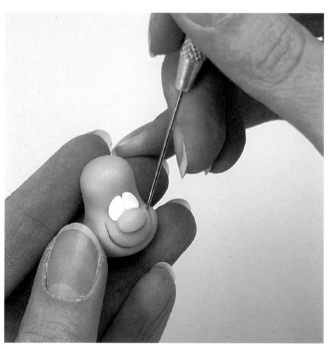

Step 7. Then add the smile with a small needle tool.

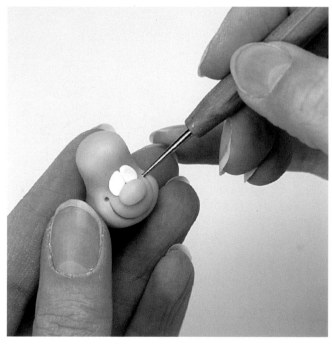

Step 8. Use the end of the stylus to add a finished look to both sides of the smile.

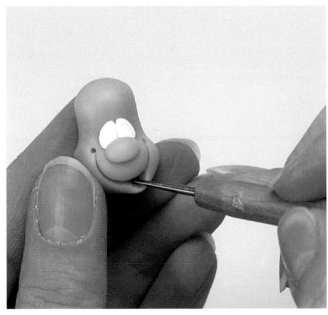

Step 9. If you choose to have an opening in the mouth, insert the stylus and gently pull the clay down.

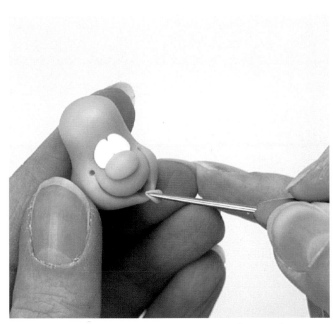

Step 10. Then insert a small pink tongue into the mouth opening with a needle tool.

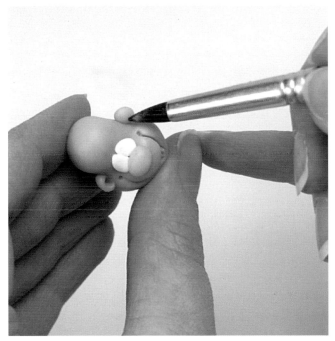

Step 11. To make the ears, roll two balls of flesh clay. Hold the first ball to the side of the face. Attach with the blending tool by inserting it into the center of the ball and pushing the clay into the side of the head. Do the same on the other side.

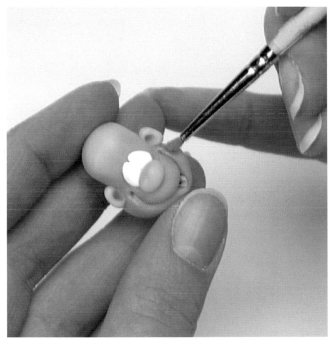

Step 12. Last, with a small brush add blush to the cheeks and the top of the nose.

Alternate Face Method

Step 1. A round head like the one on the angel needs an indent for the eyes to lie in. Otherwise the eyes will protrude too far from the head. To make the indent, I use the handle end of the knife.

Paint the Eyes

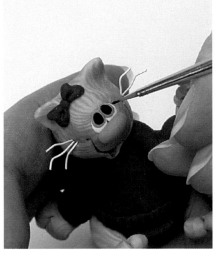

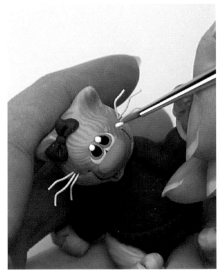

Step 2. For the eyes, first select the color you want to use for the iris. Use a small round brush to paint on the color. Use the shape of the eye as a guide, leaving white showing at the bottom.

Step 3. The black paint is next. This time use the colored part of the eye as a guide to paint the black. Try to leave an even amount of color all the way around the black.

Step 4. The character seems to come to life when the white accent is added to each eye. After the paint has dried, add two to three coats of gloss varnish to the entire eye. It protects the paint from getting scratched off and adds a touch of realism.

CLAY COLORS FOR THE FACE

In the supplies list for most projects, I list white and pink clays—even if they are not specifically used in the step by step demonstration—because you will need them to make the eyes and mouth.

Make the Arms and Hands

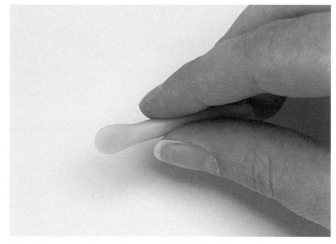

Step 1. Make each arm from a ⁷⁄₁₆" (1.1cm) flesh clay ball. Roll the ball into a 1¼" (3.2cm) long log. Flatten ¼" (.64cm) of the bottom of the log. This will become the hand.

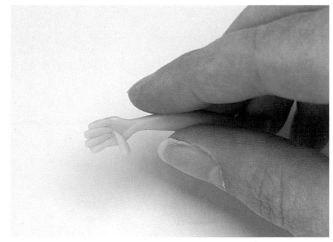

Step 2. Make the fingers and thumbs from ⅛" (.32cm) balls of clay formed into ¼" (.64cm) long teardrops. Place four teardrops on the palm of the hand so the rounded ends are visible from the other side. Place the thumb on the side of the hand.

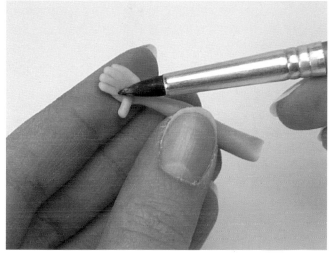

Step 3. Use the blending tool to blend the points of the teardrops into the palm of the hand.

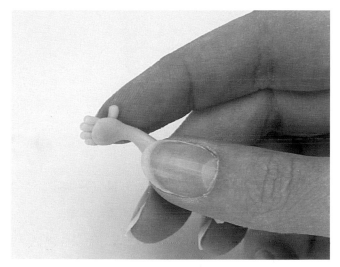

Step 4. The top side of a hand should look like this.

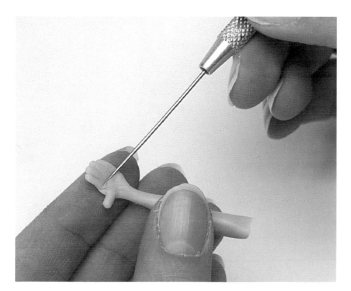

Step 5. The needle tool can also be used to make an impression on the palm where the hand would naturally crease.

ARM AND HAND SIZING

The sizes for the arms and hands shown here are standard for all projects. However, the angel (Amore) and witch (Celeste) should be made just a little bit bigger.

Make the Legs and Feet

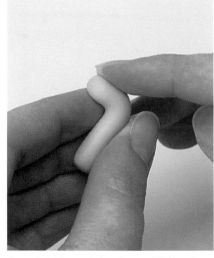

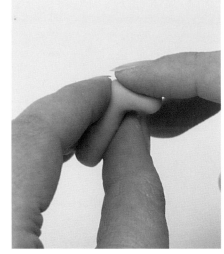

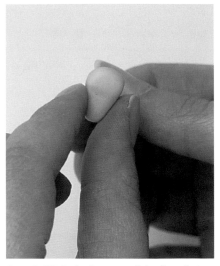

Step 1. Make each leg from a ¾" (2cm) ball rolled into a 1¾" (4.5cm) log. Bend the end of the log up to create the foot.

Step 2. Roll the ankle gently between your finger and thumb. Use your fingers to gently pinch the heel a little.

Step 3. With the bottom of the foot facing you, pinch the bottom part of the heal so that the foot tapers at the bottom.

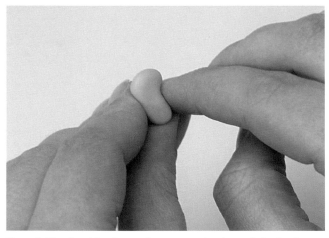

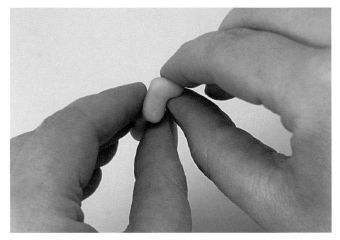

Step 4. Use the side of your finger to make the arch in the foot.

Step 5. Pinch the top of the foot just a little. Don't forget to make a right foot and a left foot!

LEG AND FEET SIZING

The sizes for the legs and feet shown here are standard for all projects.

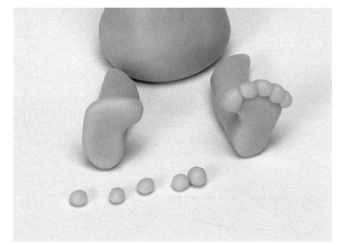

Step 6. Add the toes last. Make each big toe from a ³⁄₁₆" (.48cm) ball and each small toe from a ⅛" (.32cm) ball. Put the big toe on first, then the four little ones.

Skinner Blend

Many creative things can be done with a Skinner Blend, from making beautiful cane components to wonderful backgrounds. This technique was developed and published by Judith Skinner, hence the name Skinner Blend. A Skinner Blend can be made with a number of different colors, but for this example we will use only two.

Step 1. Begin with two triangles of color. Place them together using the picture as a guide.

Fold in half.

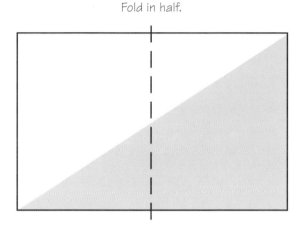

Step 2. Following the diagram, fold the slabs of clay in half.

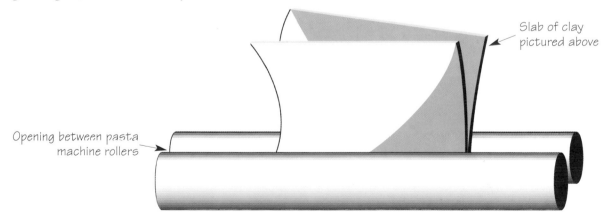

Slab of clay pictured above

Opening between pasta machine rollers

Step 3. Place the clay in the pasta machine with the fold going into the rollers first. The end corners will meet to form a square. I angled the back half of the rectangle in the diagram so that you would be able to see how the ends meet colorwise. Repeat this process about twenty-five times to get a smooth blend. It is important that you put the clay in the pasta machine in the same direction each time.

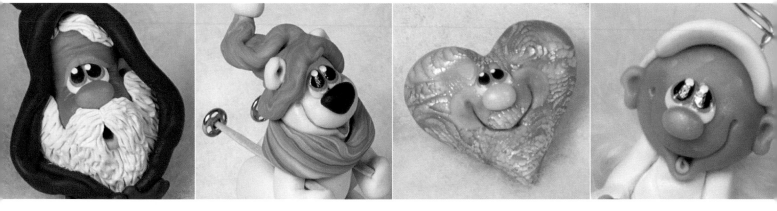

JOLLY OLD ST. NICK   SHIVERS   THROB   AMORE

BLIZZARD

winter

I could write a whole book about wintertime alone. Wintertime, especially Christmas, is where I often draw my creativity from. Like most people, I adore everything about the holidays, particularly the extra warmth that people seem to have toward each other (despite the chilly weather). It is not unusual to hear "Jingle Bells" chiming out from my studio in the middle of the summer! Re-creating some of the same feelings that I have during my favorite time of year may be one of the reasons why my characters, for the most part, are always happy.

Jolly Old St. Nick

Santa is a great project to start with. This project will give you some practice making a face, although it does not have to be formed perfectly, because the beard will cover most of it. By adding simple texturing to a project, you can create a great amount of detail.

I first learned to make a hood like the one on this Santa, from Maureen Carlson. She has a wonderful collection of teaching videotapes available, including one on creating Santas.

Once you have made the Santa pin, experiment with other flat-backed faces. Try making ladies with scarves or flowers wrapped around their faces, different period costume hats, etc. You can also turn Santa into a wizard simply by changing his hood to a metallic blue color, eliminating the holly and adding a star to the tip of his hood. The possibilities are endless!

SUPPLIES
- *clay colors:* red, flesh, white, green, pink
- basic tools (page 9)

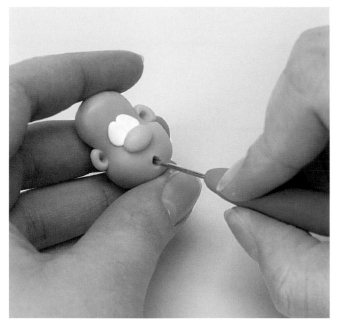

Step 1. Santa's Face. Make the face from a 1" (2.5cm) flesh clay ball. After making the face (see page 13), lay it down on the table with the front of the face up, and push slightly on the edges to make the back flat while still maintaining the roundness of the top. After making the face, instead of making a smile, insert the needle tool ¼" (.64cm) under the nose and pull it down. Gently rock it back and forth to create a teardrop opening for the mouth. Set the face aside.

Step 2. Beard and Mustache. Starting with a ¾" (1.9cm) white ball, create a teardrop shape by pinching the side of the ball between your thumb and finger. Then flatten to ⅛" (.32cm) thick.

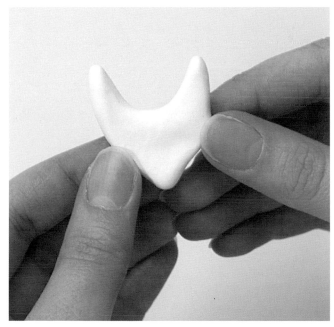

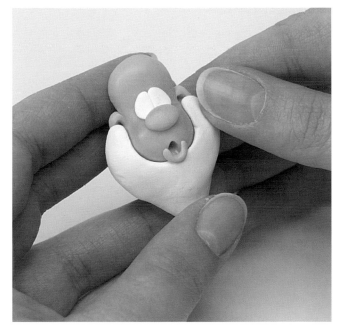

With your finger, indent the wide end of the teardrop, forming a U, to create the beard shape. If you need to, you can gently pull on the sides so that they will reach the edge of the ears..

Attach the beard to the face. Curve a very small roll of flesh-pink clay and attach it to the mouth for his bottom lip.

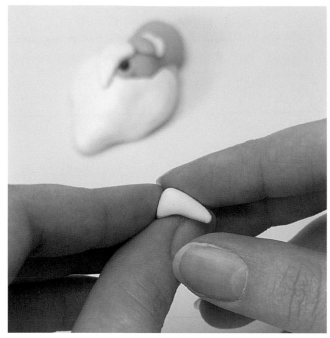

Each side of the mustache starts as a ⅜" (.95cm) white clay ball. Start with a teardrop shape and pinch the wide end slightly. The fat end goes under the nose.

Step 3. Texture the Beard. Hold the needle tool at a 45° angle, instead of straight up and down, when pulling it through the clay. This will give you better lines in his beard. Texture the beard by slowly dragging the needle tool through the clay several times. Stop when you like how it looks.

Step 4. Add Face Detail. Each eyelid is a ⅛" (.32cm) ball of flesh clay. Make each ball a very skinny teardrop. With the wide ends toward the center, place the teardrop above the eyes.

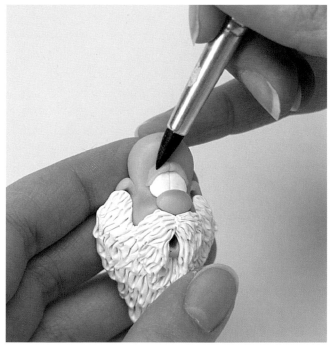

A tapered-end clay shaper helps to easily blend the edges of the eyebrows into his face.

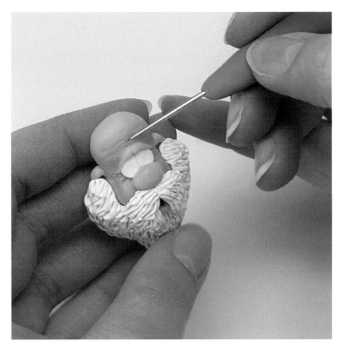

The needle tool is used to make a few wrinkles on his forehead and at the corners of his eyes.

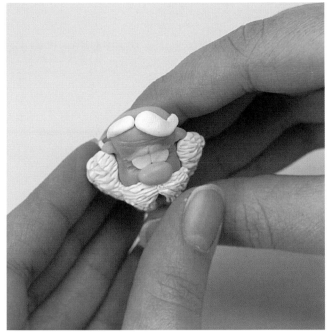

Use two small white clay balls, $3/16"$ (.48cm) and $1/4"$ (.64cm), to make Santa's bangs. Make two teardrops and attach them to the top of his forehead. Again, use the needle tool to texture his hair. Set aside.

Step 5. Make the Hood. For his hood, make a 5" × 2" (12.7cm × 5.1cm) red clay rectangle, $1/32"$ (0.8mm) thick (no. 5 on your pasta machine). Holding each corner of one long side, join the corners and pinch the sides together to form a seam.

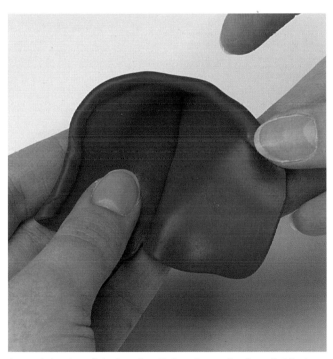

Around the rim of the hood, roll the edge under for a finished look.

Hint After working with red clay, wash your hands thoroughly. Otherwise, the very strong pigment will stay on your hands and rub off onto the next color you use.

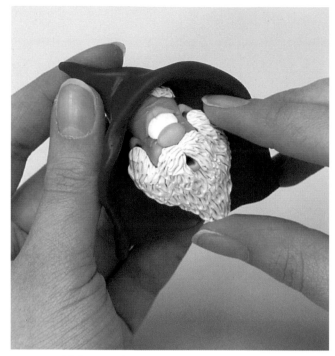

Step 6. Add the Hood. After washing your hands to remove the red residue, place the face inside the hood.

Form the hood around Santa's face. Pull the tip of the hood over to the side and arrange.

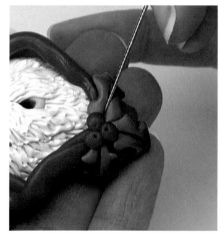

Step 7. Make the Holly. Cut three holly leaves from a ⅛" (.32cm) thick slab of green clay (number one on your pasta machine).

Smooth the edges of the leaves and arrange them at the bottom of the hood. Add three small red berries to the middle of the holly.

With a smaller needle tool, add lines to the holly.

Blizzard Pin

Most of my favorite tools are the ones that I have made or that are found objects. I now enjoy going to the hardware store with my husband, because I consider it a challenge to find new things to use with polymer clay. For example, a finishing nail, when pressed through a flat ornament, makes a perfect-sized hole for a string. The following are just a few examples of things that can be used as tools or for texturing clay:

- straws
- old toothbrushes
- cookie cutters
- candy molds
- lace
- knitting needles
- textured rolling pins
- decorative-edged scissors
- paper punches

If you do not have a heart paint stick like the one in the step-by-step photo, you can easily make your own. Here's how:

1. Form a slab of clay ⅝" (1.6cm) thick.
2. Use a ¼" (.65cm) heart Kemper cutter to cut out a heart.
3. Gently press the heart on the table so it is flat. Bake.
4. Press the heart into the clay as is, or add a handle to it and rebake it.

A three-point needle tool can be a great time-saver if you plan to make any eyelet lace from clay or anything else needing three dots. Here is how to make one:

1. Find or buy three needles that are the same size. I used larger needles found in the embroidery section of the store.
2. Roll a scrap piece of clay into a log. Make it a size that will be comfortable for you to hold.
3. Insert the needles one at a time into the end of the log. I have them in a triangle pattern, but you can design it however you like.
4. You will probably need to roll the clay around the needles.
5. Bake.

SUPPLIES

- *clay colors:* pearl white, white, pink
- basic tools (page 9)
- pattern on page 28
- heart paint stick (or handmade tool)
- blue eye shadow
- glitter paint
- three-point needle tool

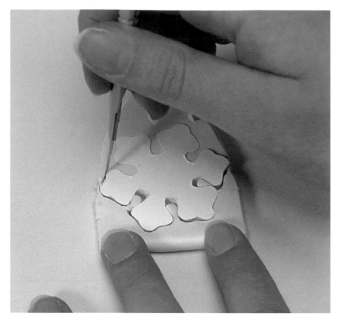

Pattern for snowflake

Step 1. Snowflake Cutout. Trace the snowflake pattern onto a piece of card stock or posterboard and cut out. Run pearl white clay through the pasta machine on the no. 2 setting and fold in half. When you fold the clay in half, start at the fold and gently slide your finger across the top sheet as you lay it down to help prevent air from getting trapped between the two sheets. Place the pattern on top of the clay slab. Using a dull scalpel or knife, trace around the pattern in a continuous motion to cut it out.

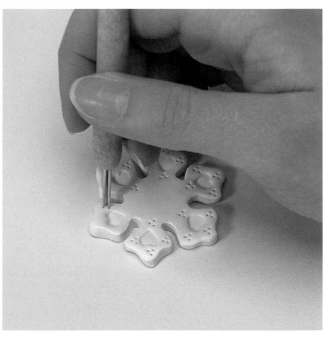

Step 2. Details. Peel the pattern off the clay. Pick the snowflake up and smooth all of the edges with your fingers. Use the paint stick or handmade tool to emboss a heart shape into each extension of the snowflake.

With the three-point needle tool, make the pattern on the snowflake, using the picture as a guide. If you have not made this tool, just use your regular needle tool to make the set of three dots.

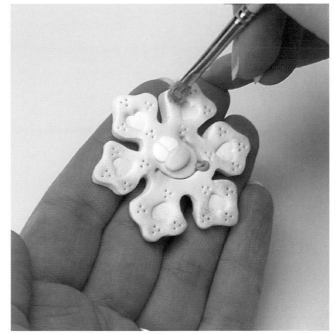

Step 3. Face. Put the face in the middle of the snowflake. Add blush to the cheeks.

Using a different brush, apply blue eye shadow or powder to the three sides of each extension. Do not add it around the face. Bake according to manufacturer's directions.

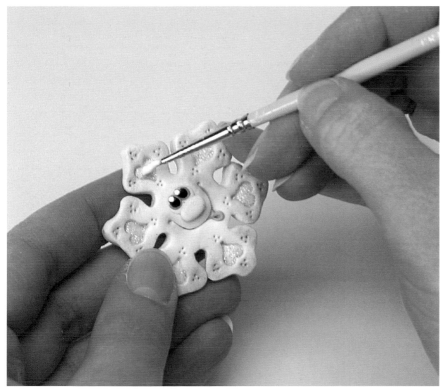

To make an ornament
Enlarge the pattern, run it through number one on your pasta machine, and push a hole through the top of the snowflake.

Step 4. Finish. After the snowflake has baked and cooled, paint the eyes and seal them. Paint the iridescent glitter paint into each of the embossed hearts.

Shivers

Often times you may want to make a larger project without using all of your clay to do it. You can save clay by covering with clay other objects such as

- wood
- glass
- metal
- paper towels
- aluminum foil
- wire mesh
- masking tape
- newspaper
- cardboard
- factory-formed papier maché
- light switch plates

Look at recyclables, such as glass or cans, and think of creative ways to cover them. I have also found cheap objects to cover at garage sales, flea markets and dollar stores. A base can also be created by covering scrap clay with the good stuff. When you cover an object with clay, do not trap any air between the clay and the object being covered. Trapped air can cause a piece to crack when it is baked. Also watch out for air bubbles. Another way to handle trapped air in a ball of aluminum foil, for example, is to make a small pinprick in a concealed area to allow the air to escape during baking.

SUPPLIES
- *clay colors:* white, blue, black, pink, silver
- basic tools (page 9)
- extra aluminum foil
- glitter paint
- two metal snaps

Important Note Styrofoam products should never be used in the oven because they can release harmful fumes. Also, children should always check with an adult before putting anything in the oven.

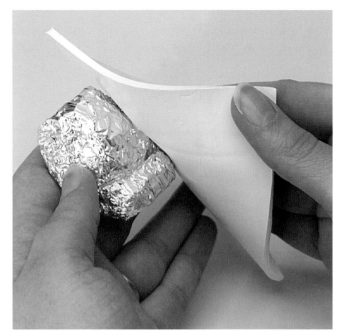

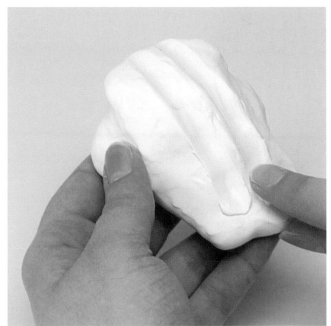

Step 1. Snowy Slope. Crumple a piece of scrap aluminum foil to about 1" (2.5cm) at the highest end, by 2" (5.1cm) wide by 1½" (3.8cm) long. Make a large sheet of white clay (run through the pasta machine on the no. 1 setting).

Cover the aluminum foil with the clay and mold clay into the shape of a slope. Use your finger to press two ski indentations down the slope. They should be about the same distance apart as the skis will be on the bear. Dimensions of the covered slope are 1½" (3.8cm) at the highest point by 3" (7.6cm) wide by 3½" (8.9cm) long.

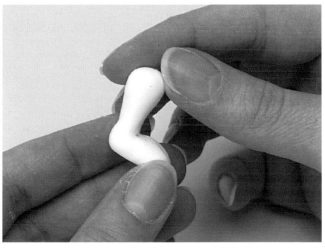

Step 2. Bear's Body. Use a ⅞" (2.2cm) ball of white clay for the bear's body. Shape it into a fat teardrop, and push the point back (refer to picture). This is done to make him look as though he is leaning forward.

Step 3. Legs. Create each leg from an ¹¹⁄₁₆" (1.7cm) ball of white clay. Roll each ball into a 1¼" (3.2cm) long snake of clay, and bend the foot up. The foot needs to be thick enough to support the bear's body in a standing position.

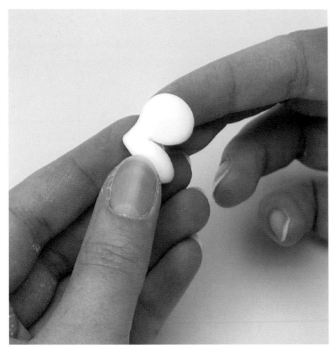

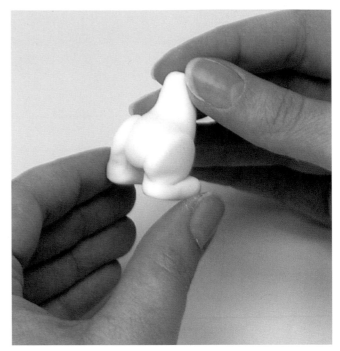

Pinch the leg and form it into a semi-flat circle and bend it forward a little. Do the same to the other leg.

Simulataneously attach both legs toward the back of the body.

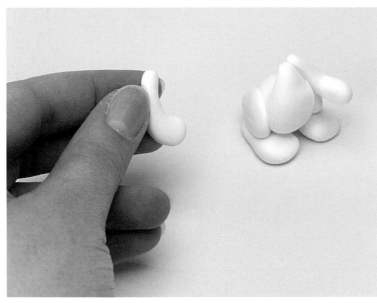

Step 4. Arms. Make each arm from a ½" (1.3cm) white clay ball. Shape it into a tapered log and flatten slightly between your fingers. Gently bend the wide end forward. Put enough curve in his paws so he can hold his ski poles.

Make sure that he can stand on his own. You might have to move his body a little to do this. Insert two pieces of wire into his neck to support the head.

Step 5. Head. Create his head from a ¾" (1.9cm) white clay ball. Roll half the ball between your thumb and finger to create a slight impression. Push the wide end of his face up just a little to form his cheeks. Slide his head onto the wires in his neck and gently push his head onto his shoulders. Add his face and use a triangular nose of black clay. Add blush.

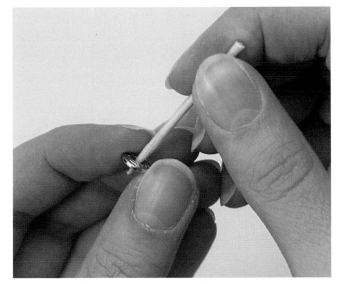

Step 6. Ski Poles. Cover an entire toothpick with white glue and let dry. Trim the toothpick, from one end only, to 1¾" (4.5cm) long. Add superglue gel to the tip of the other end of the toothpick and insert it into the hole in the middle of the snap. Repeat to make a second ski pole.

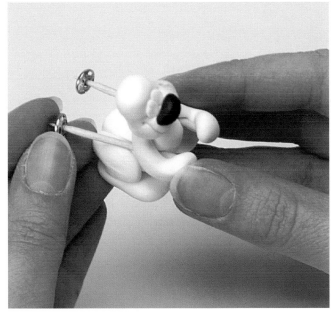

Slightly lift an arm and place the ski pole under it. The rough end of the pole should be gently pushed into his paw. Push the arm back down and press the arm into the toothpick. Repeat for the second arm.

Step 7. Hat. Mix a ½" (1.3cm) ball of blue clay with a ½" (1.3cm) ball of white clay until you have a nice marbled effect. Shape a ⅝" (1.6cm) ball of the marbled clay into a teardrop, and insert the pointed tool or the end of a paintbrush into the wide end. Roll the paintbrush back and forth to make the opening for his hat.

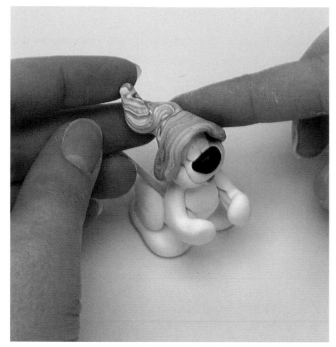

Arrange his hat around his face. Remember to angle the tip of his hat backward because he is going down a hill.

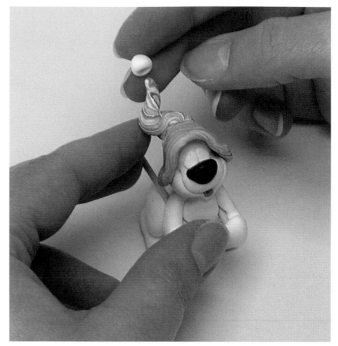

Make a ¼" (.64cm) white ball for the pom-pom at the end of his hat. With the end of a paintbrush, make a small hole in the ball and place the tip of his hat into it.

Step 8. Ears. Each ear is made from a ³⁄₁₆" (.48cm) ball of white clay. Use the clay shaper tool to make the indent in an ear while attaching it to his hat (head).

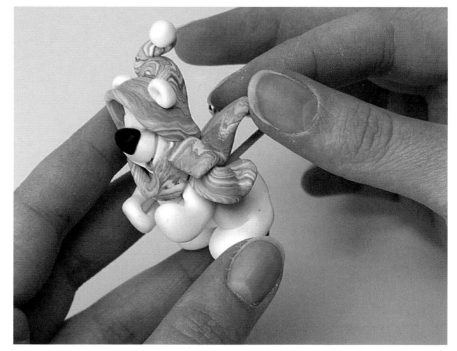

Step 9. Scarf. Roll the remainder of the blue and white marbled clay (from step 7) into a log and then flatten it between your fingers to make the scarf. Wrap it around his neck, leaving the tails off to the side toward his back. Remember to arrange them so they will look as though they are flying in the wind.

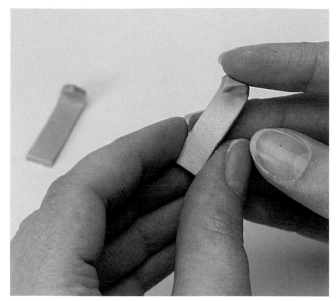

Step 10. Skis. Cut each ski from a slab of silver clay that has been run through no. 1 on the pasta machine. The ski should be about 1¾" (4.5cm) long and ¾" (1.9cm) wide. Curve the tip of each ski up a little so that it points back toward the bear.

Step 11. Assemble. Add a little bit of superglue gel to the bottom of each foot where it will touch the ski. Place him on the skis on top of the slope just to make sure that his skis fit in the grooves made in the slope. Do not forget to add his tail; make it from a ¼" (.64cm) white clay ball. Bake the bear and slope separately and according to manufacturer's directions.

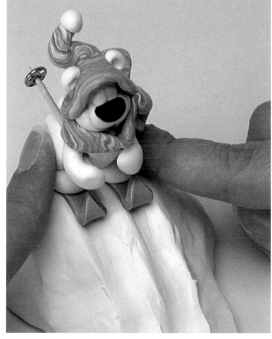

Step 12. Finishing Touches. Paint and seal his eyes. Add a little glue (either superglue or E-6000) to the bottom of each ski and then attach him to the top of the slope.

Add glitter paint to the slope, and add a couple coats of gloss sealer to the grooves in the slope.

Throb

SUPPLIES

- *clay colors:* transparent, transparent pink, white
- basic tools (page 9)
- one sheet of imitation silver leaf
- glitter
- piece of tissue paper
- burnishing tool (you can also use the underside of a spoon for this)

In this project, you will learn about Mokume Gane, the technique of stacking thin sheets of clay, distorting the layers and cutting thin slices from the multilayered stack of clay. The thin slices will show swirls of the colors used in the process. This particular form of Mokume Gane, using transparent clay and imitation metal leaf (also known as foil), was developed by Lindly Haunani. She has developed many other techniques, especially with transparent clay, and has a video explaining further techniques. You will be amazed at the depth this technique can achieve using transparent clays. Also experiment with making Mokume Gane without the imitation leaf and with layering transparent and opaque clays.

A few suggestions: When you make slices from the stack of clay, make them very thin and use a NuBlade. Flip pieces over to see which side has the best design. The composition leaf is very delicate and easily sticks to raw clay. Because it is so thin, it would be a good idea to turn off any fans around your work area before even opening the package.

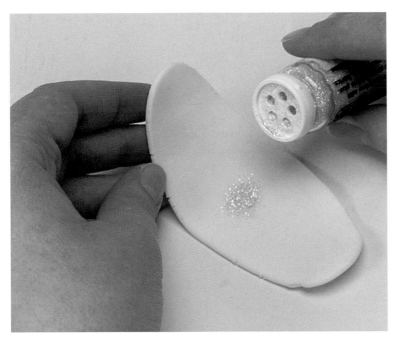

Step 1. Prepare the Clay. Start with half of a 2-ounce (56.7g) block or ball of transparent clay. Run it through the no. 1 setting on your pasta machine. (I used very fine pink glitter; you may use whatever color you want.) Add very little glitter at a time into the clay or you will end up with a mess. Sprinkle some in the middle of the slab of clay and fold it in half, creating a pocket. Push the sides together so that the glitter does not fall out. Leave the top open. Put this through the pasta machine with the folded end first. This way, any trapped air will go right out the opening. Continue this a few more times until you have as much glitter as you want evenly dispersed through the clay.

Step 2. Skinner Blend. I chose not to add glitter to the pink half. This way, when the Skinner Blend is made, the glitter will gradually fade into the pink as it is blended.

Run the two-toned slab of clay through the pasta machine to create the Skinner Blend.

Tip   To keep the sheet of clay from widening as it is repeatedly put through the pasta machine, place an unopened block of clay at the top of your rollers. This helps you to control the width that the clay becomes as it is repeatedly put through the rollers.

Step 3. Divide. Cut the sheet of clay into seven equal pieces.

Step 4. Mokume Gane Stack. Take a piece of silver leaf (imitation) out of the package. Be very careful with it as it comes apart very easily. (This would also be a good time to turn off any fans!) Lay six pieces of clay onto the foil. Press down on them or roll over them to make sure that the leaf sticks well to the clay.

Cut the pieces apart again and stack them going from lightest to darkest. Press them together firmly so they will stick to each other and to get rid of any air pockets.

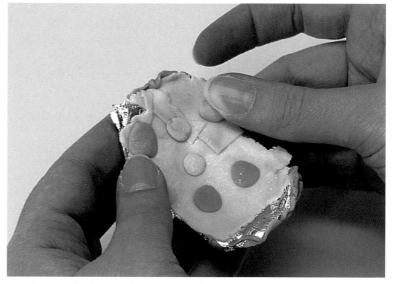

Put the seventh sheet without silver leaf on the bottom to cover the last layer of silver. Roll a few odd-shaped balls and push them into the bottom layer. From the top side it will help to create hills and valleys to take slices from, giving you a more interesting pattern.

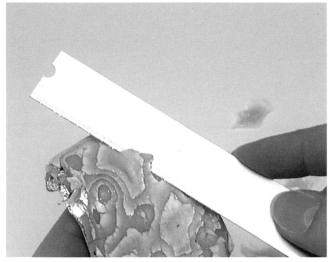

With a NuBlade, take very thin slices from the top, rotating the slab of clay as you go.

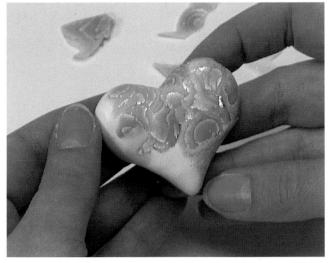

Step 5. Base. Form a heart shape out of scrap white clay. Begin adding the Mokume Gane slices until the entire heart is covered.

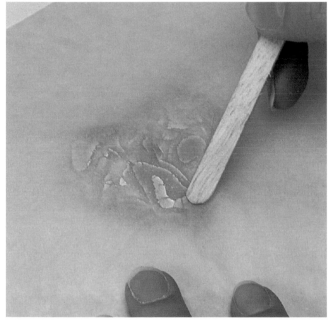

Once the heart is covered, place a piece of tissue paper over the heart and use a burnishing tool or the back of a spoon to rub all of the slices down so you will have a smooth surface.

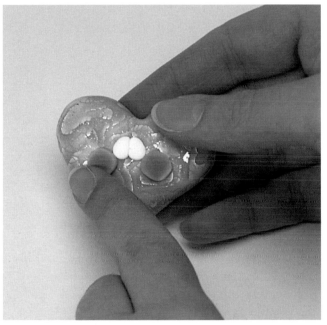

Place the eyes next to each other on the heart. The cheeks were made from leftover Skinner Blend rolled into a cane from a dark center to a light edge. Two slices from this cane create the cheeks. Place each below the eyes and off to the side a bit.

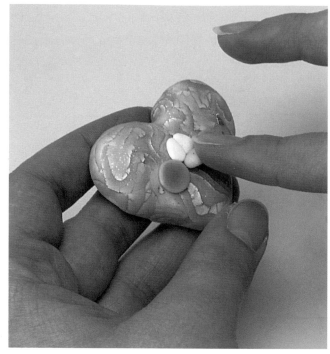

The nose is a small ball of the pink transparent placed directly under the eyes.

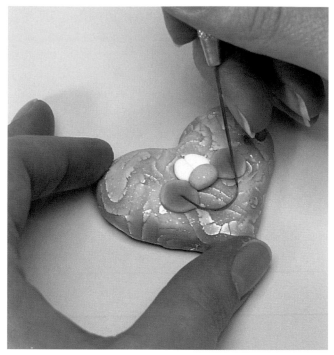

Press the needle tool into the clay starting at one cheek and pull it through the clay to the other side.

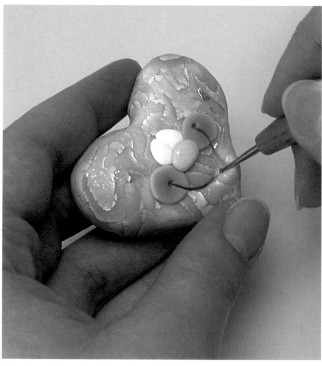

Use the wide end of the stylus to create dimples at the corners of his mouth. Also use the stylus to gently pull the mouth open.

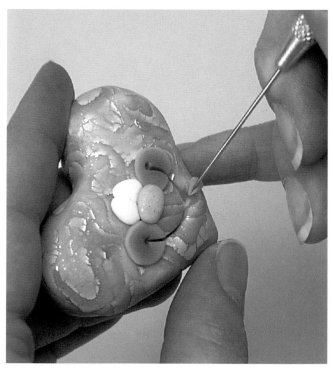

Make a small teardrop of pink transparent clay for the tongue. Use the needle tool to insert it into his mouth.

Amore

In this project, I incorporate the use of feathers. There are many craft objects that can be incorporated or used with a character. A few examples are:

- metal charms
- natural mohair/wool
- wood or bark
- stones
- terra cotta
- glass
- marbles
- shells
- paper
- cardboard
- metal
- glass beads

How you attach or include these objects depends on whether it is porous or nonporous. Porous items, such as wood and paper, can be attached with a thin layer of Sobo white glue. Nonporous objects, such as glass and metal, can be baked with the polymer clay and securely glued together with superglue gel after baking. I personally prefer to use the superglue gel (as opposed to the superglue) when attaching things because it does not run and is less likely to get on my fingers.

SUPPLIES
- *clay colors:* pearl white, red, flesh, pink, white
- basic tools (page 9)
- needle-nose pliers
- gold wire
- two white feathers

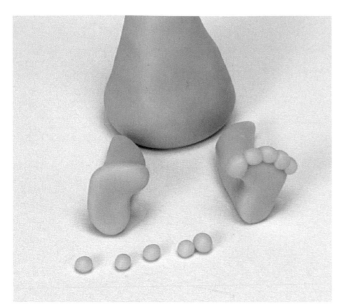

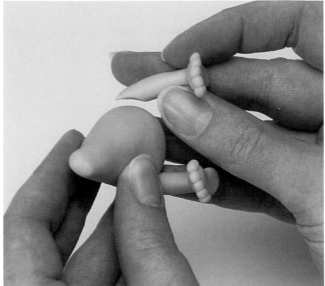

Step 1. Body and Legs. Make the angel's body from a 1⅛" (3cm) clay ball. Make each leg from a ¾" (1.9cm) ball rolled out to a 1¾" (4.5cm) long log. Each big toe is a ³⁄₁₆" (.48cm) ball, and each small toe is a ⅛" (.32cm) ball.

Trim each leg down to the size that you want. When you trim, cut the end off at an angle so that it will lay flush against the body. Attach both legs at the same time.

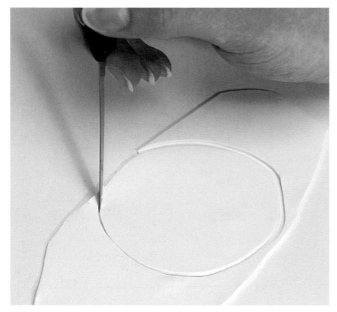

Step 2. Gown. Run a sheet of pearl white clay through the pasta machine first on no. 1, then on no. 4. Cut out a circle about 3½" (8.9cm) in diameter. The circle does not have to be perfect; once it is draped over the body, its shape will not matter.

Smooth the edges of the circle, then drape it over the angel's body. Place the point of his body in the center of the white circle and drape it down the sides of his body.

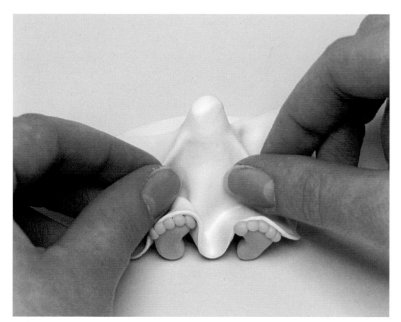

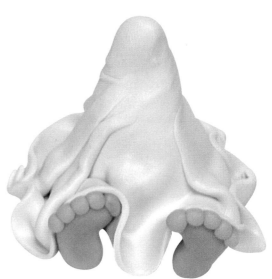

Adjust the gown around his body. Make sure to drape the gown between his feet.

Create a few twists and curls at the bottom of the gown to add some interest. Set the body aside while you make the arms.

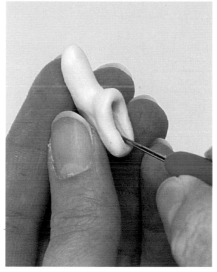

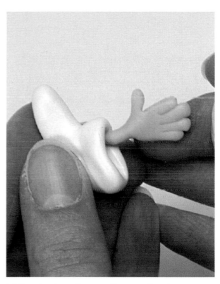

Step 3. Arms. Make each sleeve from a ⅝" (1.6cm) ball of pearl white clay. Shape it into a long teardrop and flatten it slightly with your fingers. Push the wide end up to create an **L** shape.

Push a wider needle tool into the end of the sleeve and pull it downward to create enough of an opening to insert the hand.

Make the hand according to the directions in the Basic Techniques (remember to make a left and a right). Trim the extra clay off from the wrist and insert the hand into the opening in the sleeve. Pinch the sides of the sleeve around the wrist to secure the hand.

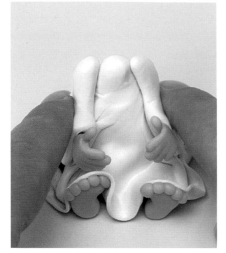

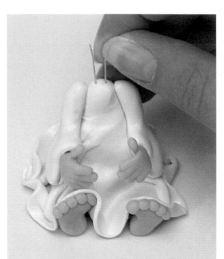

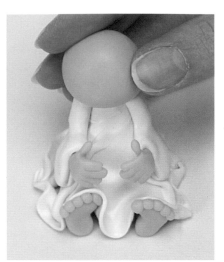

Attach both arms to the body at the same time. The shoulders should be at the same height as the top point of the body.

Step 4. Head. Insert two 1" (2.5cm) long wires into the top of the body, leaving ½" (1.3cm) sticking out of the top. This will support the head.

Tip For added durability, you can add a dab of superglue to the end of the wire before it is inserted into the body and to the other end before the head is placed on it.

The head is a 1" (2.5cm) clay ball. Push it onto the wire and gently onto the shoulders. Add his face and ears. Each eye is a ³⁄₁₆" (.48cm) white ball. Cut a ¼" (.64cm) ball in half to make two ears. The nose is ¼" (.64cm) ball.

Tip Before adding the eyes, I take the handle end of my knife and indent the clay at about the middle. This is just enough for the eyes to rest in, so that they do not bug out of his head.

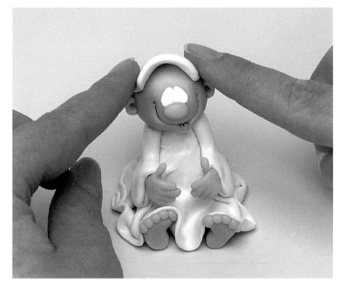

Step 5. Cap. Make his cap from a ⅝" (1.6cm) ball of pearl white clay. Flatten to about ⅛" (.32cm) thick. Using a wider needle tool, indent each side about ¼" (.64cm) into the hat. This will create the brim of the hat. Round out the rest of the hat with your fingers.

Place the cap on his head and gently press it down. The majority of the hat will cover the back of his head.

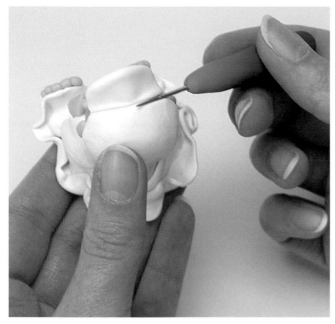

With the wider needle tool, indent the hat in the back where the brim meets the hat.

Twist a skinny rope together and place it in the indentation on the hat.

Step 6. Heart. Make a red clay heart that is about ³⁄₁₆" (.48cm) thick. Place it between his hands and wrap his fingers around it to hold onto it.

Tip When working with red and white clay, make what you need with the white clay first and then use the red. After handling the red clay, wash your hands thoroughly before using any other color. Otherwise you will have red pigment on your hands, and it will come off onto the next color.

Step 7. Halo. Make the halo from 20-gauge wire. Begin with a piece that is 3" (7.6cm) long. Bend it in half so that the two ends touch. Hold the two ends together with needle-nose pliers and twist, holding the rounded end.

Bend the halo to a 90° angle. Trim the extra off the end so that the twisted part is about ¾" (1.9cm) long. Push it into the hat just behind the brim and off to the side a little.

Step 8. Feather Wings. Pick two feathers that match each other. Dip the very tip of each feather into white glue and push it into the back of his head. Be careful not to push it all the way through to the front. Leave at least ⅛" (.32cm) between the two feathers.

DAISY MAE

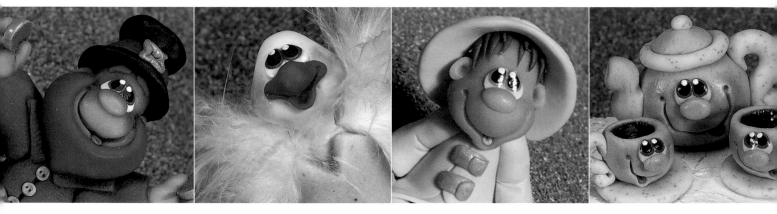

PATRICK   CHIRP   TYLER & PUDDLES   TEA FOR TWO

LUCKY

spring

Springtime is a time when everything starts fresh again. For some people it's New Year's Day, but for me, it's springtime. Trees start to bud and grow new leaves. Baby animals are born and Mother Nature begins her cycle through the seasons once again. Take this time to come up with new ideas for all seasons. Let your creativity bloom!

Lucky

SUPPLIES
- *clay colors:* green, metallic green, black, gold, white, pink
- basic tools (page 9)
- shamrock cookie cutter

This project uses a cookie cutter to form the basic shape. An amazing variety of cookie cutter shapes, both large and small, is available today. Some places even offer custom-made cookie cutters. Metal cutters work the best, but some plastic cutters also work. Remember, once you use a cookie cutter with clay, you should never use it with food products again.

Kemper cutters are similar to cookie cutters, but they are much smaller and have a small plunger in the end to extrude small pieces of clay. You can also customize some of your own shapes by reshaping ones that you have purchased. When you cut out pieces, if the clay sticks to the cutter, sprinkle some baby powder on paper or a note card. Then dip the edges of the cookie cutter in the powder, tap the side to remove any excess powder and then push it through the clay. The powder acts as a release for the clay. After you have cut out a shape, run your finger gently along the bottom edge of the clay to soften it. This will give the piece a more finished look and eliminate a sharp or rough edge after the piece has been baked.

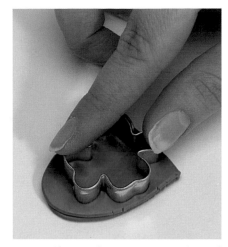

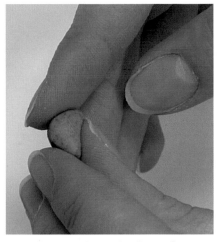

Step 1. Shamrock Cutout. Run a sheet of green clay through the pasta machine on the no. 2 setting. Fold the sheet in half, being careful not to trap any air bubbles. Use a cookie cutter to cut out the shamrock.

Step 2. Face. Smooth the edges of the shamrock and add his face. Make the eyes from ⁵⁄₁₆" (0.8cm) balls of white clay and the nose from ¼" (.64cm) ball of green.

Step 3. Hat. Make the hat from a ⁵⁄₁₆" (0.8cm) ball of metallic green clay. Flatten the ball slightly and curve it over your thumb to create the shape of a hat.

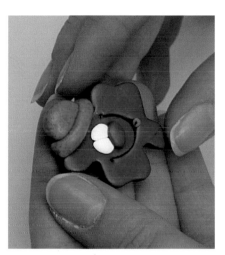

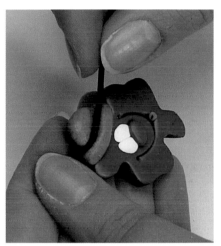

Place the top of the hat off to the side of the shamrock. Curve the hat around the edges of the shamrock.

Make the brim from a ⅛" (3.2mm) wide metallic green rope. Lay the rope at the far edge of the hat and press down just enough to secure it to the hat. Wrap the edges of the brim around the sides and cut off the excess.

Add another snake, this time out of black clay ¹⁄₁₆" (.16cm) thick. Flatten it and lay it just above the green brim.

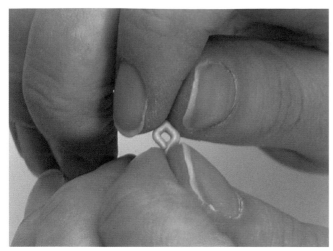

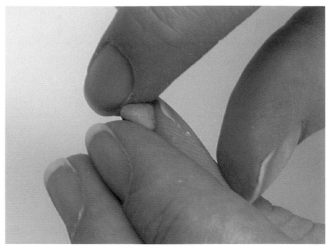

Make the gold buckle from a ⅛" (.32cm) ball of gold clay. Roll it into a snake. Pinch the two ends together, and then pinch the curved end where it was folded in half. Now pinch the other two opposite corners. You should end up with a square buckle shape. Place it in the center of the black band.

Step 4. Bow. Construct the bow from two small triangles and a tiny ball of metallic green clay. Make each half of the bow from a ³⁄₁₆" (.48cm) ball of metallic green clay. Pinch each ball into a triangle shape.

Place the first triangle so that the point is in the middle. Put the other triangle on the opposite side with its point also in the center. Place a small green ball in the center to complete the bow. You can also add folds into the bow with a needle tool, as I have done in the photo.

Step 5. Finishing Touches. After the shamrock has baked and cooled, you may add gloss varnish to the hat and bow. This will help bring out the glitter in the clay.

Patrick

This project will give you some practice making a simple armature, which is an underlying support to add strength to a figurine's form. Not all pieces will need an armature. However, if a character or project has protruding parts, such as arms or legs, an armature can help prevent the limbs from sagging, cracking or breaking. Although a piece of clay may stay in position without an armature while you are working on it, once the clay is heated in the oven, it has a tendency to droop or move a little out of position if it is not supported. A simple armature can be created out of several things, including:

- cloth-covered floral wire
- toothpicks
- wood dowels
- wire mesh
- brass rods
- telephone wire
- crumpled aluminum foil

SUPPLIES

- *clay colors:* FIMO Classic Leaf Green, FIMO Soft Tropical Green, FIMO Soft Emerald, gold, orange, flesh, pink, black, white
- basic tools (page 9)

Step 1. Base. Start with a 1½" (3.8cm) ball of Leaf Green for the base. Flatten to about ³/₁₆" (.48cm) thick. To add a little texture, pounce an old toothbrush (dedicated to clay only) around on the clay slab.

Step 2. Pot o' Gold. Make the pot for the "pot o' gold" from a 1½" (3.8cm) ball of black. Using the rounded end of one of your tools, hollow out an indentation about ½" (1.3cm) deep from the top. This is where the leprechaun's body will be nestled.

Make the rim of the pot from a ¼" (.64cm) thick black snake. Make sure that you start the rim in the back of your piece. Wrap it around and then cut off the excess when it touches the other end.

Step 3. Body. Make the body from a ⅞" (2.2cm) ball of Tropical Green formed into a fat teardrop shape. Place the wide end of the tear drop into the indentation you created in the pot.

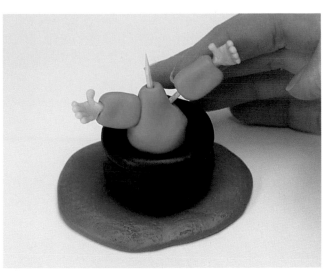

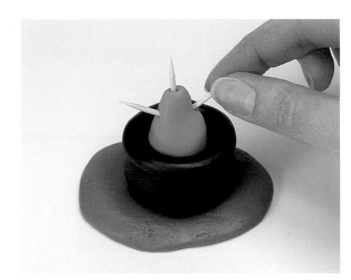

Step 4. Armature. Since the leprechaun's arms are raised into the air, they need to be supported by an armature. For a very simple armature, insert three cut toothpicks, each about 1" (2.5cm) in length, into the body. One is for the head (an alternative to using wire), and one goes on each side for his arms.

The sleeves each start as a ½" (1.3cm) ball of Tropical Green clay. Make each into a cylinder shape and indent one end enough for the leprechaun's wrist. Make the hands and insert them into the sleeves. Pinch each sleeve slightly to secure to the hand. Gently slide the sleeve onto the armature. Position the hands the way you want them.

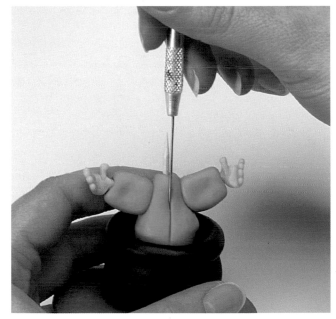

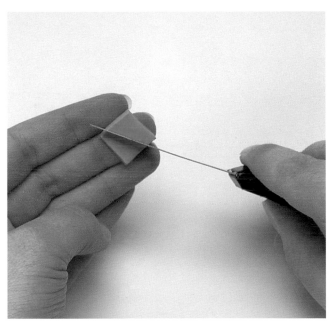

Step 5. Shirt. Use the needle tool to indent a line down the center of his body to make the shirt.

Make a ½" (1.3cm) square of Tropical Green clay from a sheet put through the pasta machine on a no. 3 setting. Cut it diagonally to make his collar.

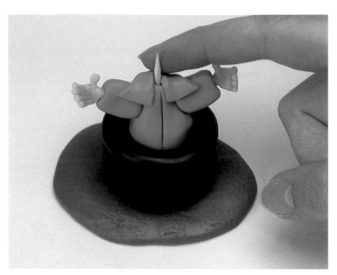

Place each side of the collar onto his body. Refer to the photo.

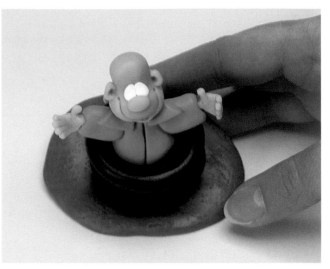

Step 6. Head. Make the head from a ¾" (1.9cm) ball of clay. Add his face.

His beard and eyebrows follow. Make the beard from a ⅝" (1.6cm) ball of orange and each eyebrow from a ⅛" (.32mm) ball of orange. Make the beard and eyebrows the same way as Santa's (see pages 23–24).

Step 7. Hat. The brim of his hat is a ½" (1.3cm) ball of Emerald. Flatten it into a circle and press it down on the top of his head.

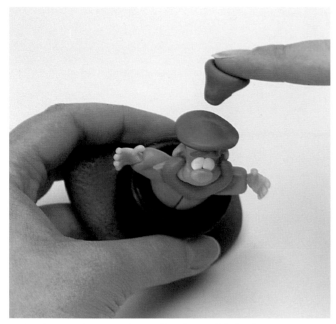

Make the top of his hat from a 9/16" (1.4cm) ball of Emerald formed into a fat teardrop shape. Flatten the rounded, wide end of the teardrop when you push the small end onto the brim.

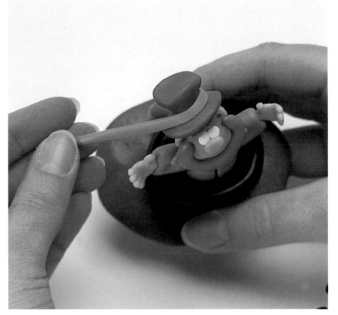

Make the band around the hat from a 1/8" (3.2cm) thick snake of Tropical Green. Flatten the snake and wrap it around the hat just above the brim.

Step 8. Finishing Touches. Add 1/16" (.16cm) balls of gold clay to the front of his jacket for buttons. Place them right on the seam and use the wide stylus to push them on.

Make the gold buckle for his hat the same way that you made the one for the shamrock.

Add small slices of gold clay all around the base of his coat and add a few to the ground in front of him. Put a gold coin into each of his hands.

Chirp

Inclusions are a lot of fun to experiment with. They are most commonly used with transparent clay but can also create some interesting effects when used with opaque clay as well. FIMO Soft clay offers five colored transparent clays (red, yellow, green, blue and orange) as well as uncolored transparent. The FIMO Soft stone colors (Rose Quartz, Lapis Lazuli, Turquoise, China Jade, Jasper and Granite) are transparent clays with tiny fibers or granules added to them. Here are some ideas for inclusions:

- glitter
- shavings from pastels
- sawdust
- spices
- crayon shavings
- sand
- dirt
- tiny stones
- colored play sand
- dried flower petals
- coffee grounds
- powdered pigments
- embossing powders
- potpourri
- tiny glass beads

SUPPLIES
- *clay colors:* transparent, yellow, orange, white
- basic tools (page 9)
- crayons (pink & purple)
- two yellow feathers

Step 1. Clay Preparation. Chop small pieces of crayon on a note card. Use pink and purple crayons. Be sure to chop them fine.

Flatten a ¾" (1.9cm) ball of transparent clay. Slowly add the crayon pieces to the transparent clay.

To mix together, fold in half to create a pocket. Run this through the pasta machine with the folded end touching the rollers first. Roll through a few times and then add more of the crayon.

Once all of the crayon is added to the transparent clay, form it into an oval (egg) shape and cut a zigzag edge toward the top of the egg.

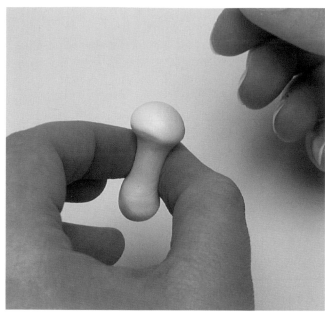

Step 2. Chick. Make the chick from a ¾" (1.9cm) ball of yellow clay. Place the ball between your fingers and roll half of the ball into a log. The top, rounded end will be his head.

Flatten the rounded end a little and shape it into a rounded triangle. This will be his head, and the other half will be the lower portion of his body.

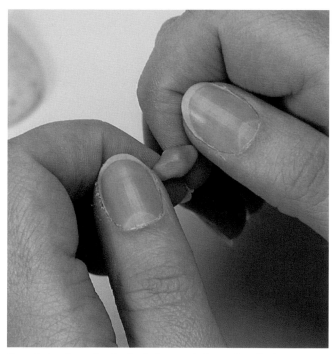

Flatten his body, but not the head, even more and press it into the back side of the egg so that the neck and head are above the zigzag cut edge. Lay the egg on your work surface, front side up, and press the edge down so that the back will be flat.

Make his eyes from a ⅛" (.32cm) white clay ball and add them to the head.

Step 3. Beak. Make the beak from a ¼" (.64cm) ball of orange clay. Use both hands and rock it back and forth between your fingers and thumbs. Essentially, you will be making an elongated diamond shape.

Pinch the sides of the diamond a little to form the corners of the beak.

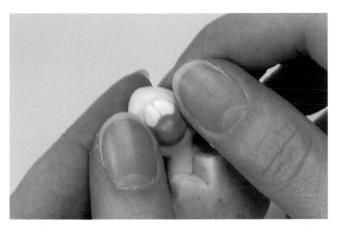

Place the beak just below his eyes. Only press down on the sides of the beak to secure it to his face.

Use a scalpel or knife to cut open his beak and create his mouth. Cut a line from one side to the other, leaving a majority of the clay on the top part of his beak.

Use the stylus to add his dimples.

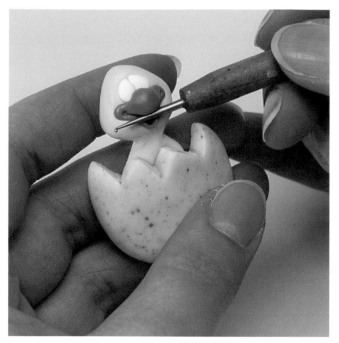

Use the stylus to open up his mouth a little by inserting it into the center of the opening and pulling the clay down a bit.

Use the side of the stylus to slightly flatten the beak's lower half.

Step 4. Feathers. Find two small yellow feathers that match, and cut them to fit the size of the chick. Generally each feather should not stick out more than 1" (2.5cm) from each side, unless that is how you want it to look. Add a little white glue to the end of one feather and gently press it into his neck, being very careful not to go all the way through. Do the other side the same way.

Tyler & Puddles

This project gives you the option (in the very last steps) of using Liquid Sculpey as a glue. Liquid Sculpey is polymer clay in a liquid form. The opaque form, white, is just referred to as Liquid Sculpey. The transparent form is known as Translucent Liquid Sculpey (TLS). At this time it can only be bought through mail-order sources.

Liquid Sculpey can be used for many different things, but in this instance we will discuss its use as a glue for raw (unbaked) clay. It becomes hard when it is baked, just as regular clay does, and will hold two pieces of clay together better than glue. It will only work like glue if it is baked, because air alone will not cure it. This gives you the freedom to move a piece around after attaching it, because Liquid Sculpey is not permanent until it has been cured in the oven. Liquid Sculpey can be applied with a toothpick, glue syringe or an old brush.

SUPPLIES
- *clay colors:* blue, white, yellow, silver, brown, pink, flesh, orange
- basic tools (page 9)
- pattern on page 62
- Liquid Sculpey (optional)

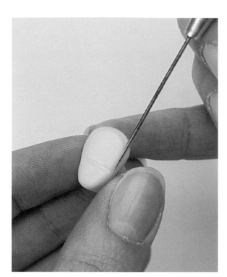

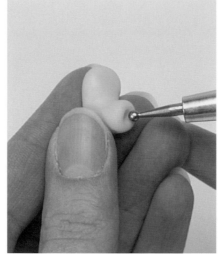

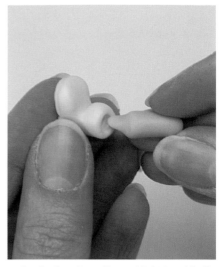

Step 1. Body and Boots. To make Tyler's body, roll a ¾" (1.9cm) ball of yellow clay. Form a fat teardrop and press the wide end down on the work surface. To form the boot shape, roll two ½" (1.3cm) yellow balls into two logs. For each leg, bend one end up to form an **L** shape. Flatten the toe end and give the back a little pinch to form the heel. To make the sole on the boot, use the needle tool to indent around the edge of the boot about ¹⁄₁₆" (.16cm) up from the bottom. Make an indent across the bottom of the boot for the heel.

Use the wide stylus to create an indentation at the top of the boot. This is where you will attach the leg.

Make the legs by rolling a ½" (1.3cm) ball of flesh clay to ¼" (.64cm) by 1½" (3.8cm). Cut two pieces ¾" (1.9cm) long. Taper each rounded end to fit into the boot. Cut the other end of each leg at a 45° angle and attach to the body.

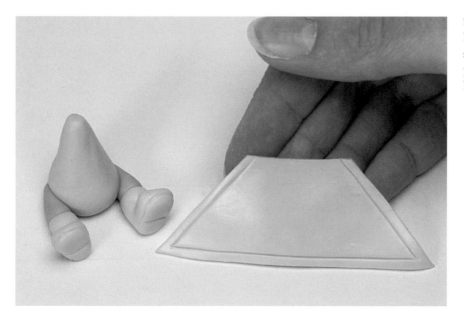

Step 2. Raincoat. Roll a 1" (2.5cm) yellow ball ³⁄₆₄" (.12cm) thick or use the no. 4 setting on a pasta machine. Lay the coat pattern on the clay and cut it out with the knife.

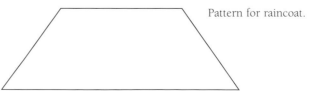

Pattern for raincoat.

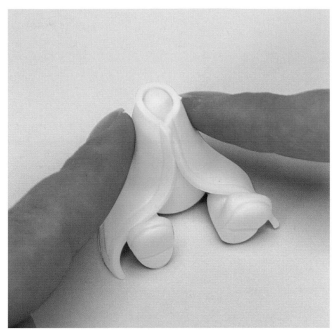

Wrap the coat around his body so the ends meet in the center front of his body. Open the bottom half of his coat outward.

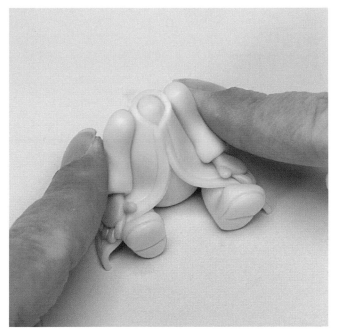

Step 3. Sleeves. For sleeves, roll two ½" (1.3cm) yellow balls into a tapered cone shape. With the stylus, indent ¼" (.64cm) at the wide end of each sleeve for a hand to be inserted. Make the hands and insert each into the end of a sleeve. Press both arms onto his body at the same time. Do not forget to make the crease marks in his arms.

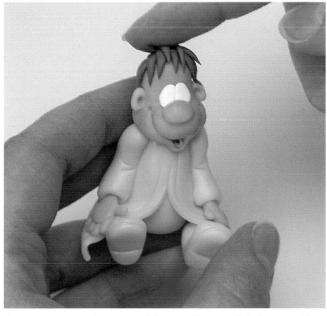

Step 4. Head. Make the head from a ¾" (1.9cm) flesh clay ball, shaped into a pear shape. Pinch the bottom of his head slightly to form his chin. Place wire into his body and slide his head onto it.

Create his face using two ⅛" (.32cm) white clay balls for eyes, a ¼" (.64cm) ball for his nose, and two ³⁄₁₆" (.48cm) balls for his ears. Add blush to the cheeks. For his hair, roll ⅛" (.32cm) brown balls into teardrops. Press the wide end of each teardrop into the top of his head.

Step 5. Hat. For the brim, flatten a ⅝" (1.6cm) yellow ball into a 1½" (3.8cm) diameter circle. Center it on his head and press down gently.

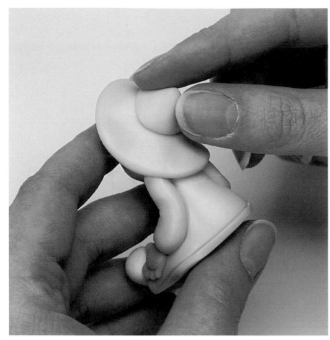

For the top of the hat, form a ⅜" (.95cm) yellow ball into a pointed dome shape. Press it onto the center of the brim. Be careful not to squish his face in the process.

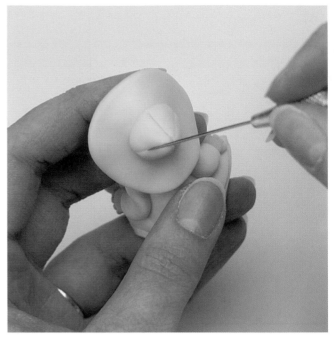

Use the needle tool to indent crossed lines into his hat to add a little detail.

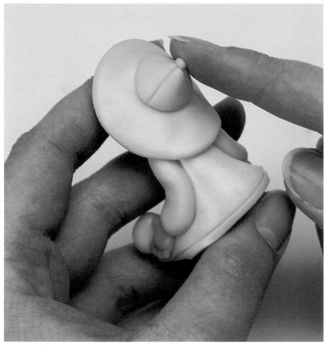

Make a ⅛" (.32cm) yellow ball and place it in the center of the lines in the hat to finish it.

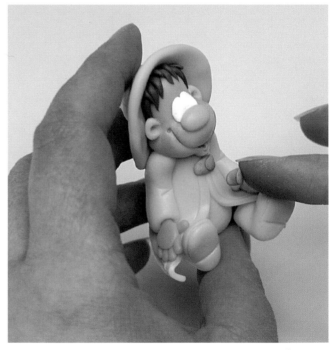

Step 6. Buckles. Make the buckles on his coat from two ³⁄₁₆" (.48cm) balls of silver clay. Roll each into a small log and flatten. Bend one end up and fold it so that it will touch the middle of the flattened log. Press both of them onto his coat in the center.

Step 7. Water Puddle. Marble together a 1" (2.5cm) white ball and a ¼" (.64cm) blue ball. Stop mixing when many stripes of color are throughout. Form the clay into a puddle shape and set it aside.

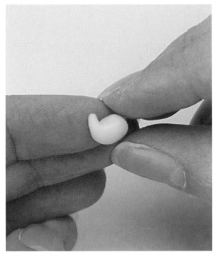

Step 8. Duck. For the duck's body, form a ¼" (.64cm) yellow ball into a crescent shape.

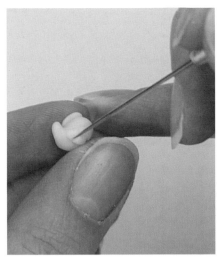

For his wings, form two ⅛" (.32cm) yellow balls into teardrops, and place one on each side with the narrow end pointing to his tail. Indent the wings with the needle tool.

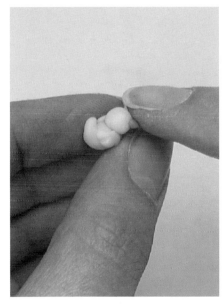

Make his head from a ³⁄₁₆" (.48cm) ball of yellow. Press it onto his body. Make the beak from a tiny orange ball shaped into a cone. Press the wide end of the cone onto his face.

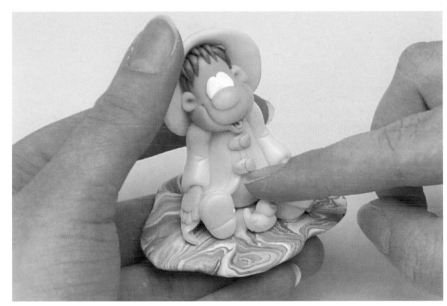

Step 9. Finish. Use a sparing amount of white glue or Liquid Sculpey on the bottom of the boy and the duck. Glue and/or attach them onto the puddle and then bake.

Daisy Mae

In this project you will learn to make two simple millefiori canes. A millefiori cane is a long log of clay that has a design going all the way through it that can only be seen on the ends. The cane, once constructed, can be reduced and sliced. The image will reduce and continue to run through the length of the cane. So many things can be done with canes. You can cover just about anything with slices of canes, make candies to decorate faux gingerbread houses and create an array of different jewelry pieces, to name a few. Several books and videos give directions for making different styles of canes, from simple canes to very complex ones.

SUPPLIES

- *clay colors:* white, yellow, green, black, terra cotta, pink
- basic tools (page 9)

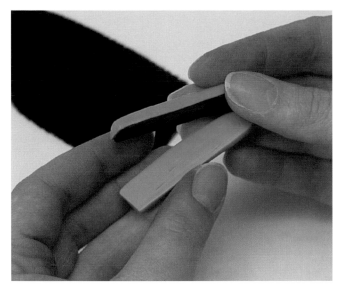

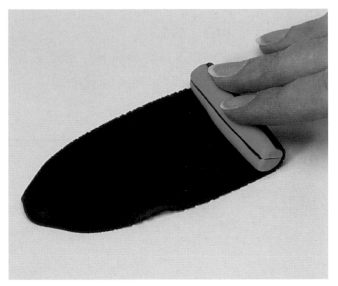

Step 1. Simple Leaf Cane. To make a simple leaf cane, start by rolling a ⅞" (2.2cm) green ball into a 2½" (6.4cm) long by ⁷⁄₁₆" (1.1cm) wide log. Use the NuBlade to divide the log in half (long way). Roll a sheet of black clay through the no. 5 setting on the pasta machine. Lay one half of the log on the black sheet, flat side down. Press on the top of the green gently so the black will stick to it. Use the knife or NuBlade to trim the black clay around the green log. Now place the half of the log with the black on it on top of the other half (refer to picture). You should now have a log with a black stripe down the center of it.

Cut a straight edge on the remaining black sheet. Lay the green log at the edge of the black sheet. Roll the log in the black sheet, being careful not to overlap the black. Watch out for air bubbles too.

This is what the cane should look like when it is finished. Do not be discouraged if the end looks a little distorted at first. Once you slice off a piece from the end, you will have a better idea of what the rest of the cane really looks like.

Step 2. Simple Flower Cane. To make the flower petals, repeat the steps for the leaf cane, using a ⅞" (2.2cm) ball of white rolled into a log 2½" (6.4cm) long by ⁷⁄₁₆" (1.1cm) wide. Instead of making the center black sheet of clay go all the way across, make it go only halfway. Also make a yellow cane that is just a ⅝" (1.6cm) yellow ball made into a log 1" (2.5cm) long by ⅜" (.95cm) wide, then wrap it in black clay. Don't add a line in the center of this one.

Reduce the flower petal cane to ³⁄₁₆" (.48cm) in diameter by gently rolling it on the table. Cut six 1½" (3.8cm) long pieces. Reduce the yellow cane to the same size as well and cut one piece 1½" (3.8cm) long.

Step 3. Cane Assembly. Assemble the flower petal canes around the yellow middle. Make sure that the black line in the petal is on the inside next to the yellow center on all of the pieces. Also check to make sure that they are that way at the other end too. Sometimes when a cane is being reduced, it can get turned in the middle.

Step 4. Cane Reducing. Because we want to maintain the shape of the petals, do not roll the cane on the table to reduce it. (That would result in a round cane instead of a flower-shaped edge.) Instead, gently and slowly stretch it. Use both hands to keep turning the piece as you do this.

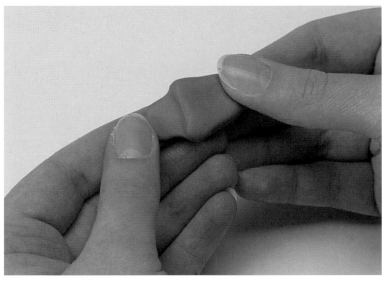

Step 5. Flowerpot. The flowerpot is made from a ¾" (1.9cm) terra cotta ball. Form the shape of a plant pot. At the top of the pot, pull a small amount of clay upward. This will be where the cane slices are added.

Tip   It is better to have a solid piece of clay for the pin back to rest on instead of many small pieces put together.

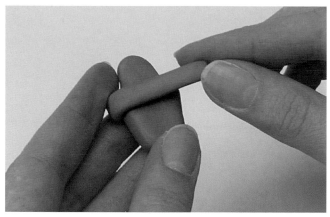

Make the brim of the flowerpot from a ⁷⁄₁₆" (1.1cm) terra cotta ball rolled out to a 1½" (3.8cm) long log and slightly flattened with your finger. Attach the brim starting at one side and wrapping around to the other side.

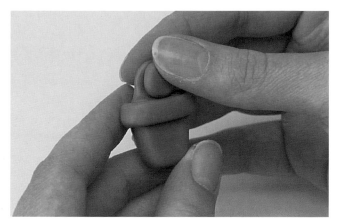

If the top part that was pulled from the pot is a little too flat to add the flower slices, add a small ball of clay and flatten it slightly. Add his face.

Step 6. Flowers and Leaves. Before slicing any of the leaf cane, pinch one side of it to shape it into a leaf. This is much easier to do before you cut it, but it can also be done after. Begin placing flower slices and leaf slices all over the extra clay at the top of the pot.

It is ready to bake when you are satisfied with how the flowers look.

Tea for Two

I was first inspired to use fabric with clay when I was introduced to some of Shelly Comiskey's wonderful characters. Although I do not know how to sew yet, I love to look at material and dream of what I will make when I do learn to sew. However, now I can use some of my favorite fabric prints with the clay— no sewing required!

When the clay and the material are put through the pasta machine together on the no. 6 setting (⅟₆₄" or the thickness of a sheet of paper), the clay is forced into the weave of the fabric. The clay backing is thin enough that the material can be draped a number of ways. Once it is baked, it will hold the form permanently. Also the clay backing will stick to other pieces of raw clay. Using polymer clay with fabric opens many creative doors, and you do not even have to use a sewing machine.

SUPPLIES

- *clay colors:* white, transparent, pink
- basic tools (page 9)
- fabric
- lace
- brown glass paint
- extra aluminum foil
- play sand colors: green, light green, rose

Step 1. Armature. Wad up a paper towel and cover it with aluminum foil. You need to create a cylinder shape (round on the sides and flat on the top and bottom). The shape does not have to be perfect because it will be covered with clay. The size should be 1¼" (3.2cm) tall by 2½" (6.4cm) in diameter before you add the clay. Run a piece of clay (scrap clay will do) through a pasta machine on the no. 1 setting. Wrap this clay around the foil shape, making sure to cover it all. It is most important that the bottom of the cylinder sets flat on the table.

Step 2. Table Skirt. Choose a fabric with a small print you like and cut a piece 2¼" (5.7cm) by 17" (43cm). This piece should be bigger than necessary so you can trim the fabric and the clay at the same time, after they have been put through the pasta machine together. Run a piece of clay (light-colored clay if you have light fabric, dark clay if you have dark fabric) through the pasta machine on the no. 2 setting. Lay the sheet of clay on the back side of the fabric and run them through the pasta machine together on the no. 6 setting.

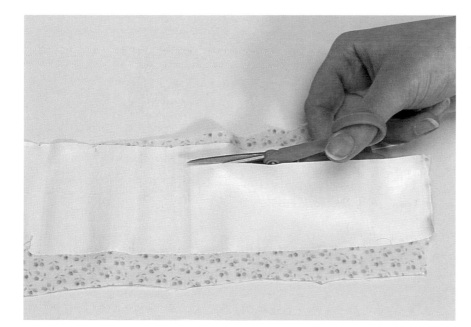

Use a pair of scissors to trim the clay-backed fabric to a piece that is 1¼" (3.2cm) by 16" (40.5cm). Note: This size may be adjusted to fit the table that you made. Make sure that you leave enough fabric to make small gathers in the table skirt. The fabric piece should be a little wider than the cylinder so that it will flare out on the bottom when gathered and attached to the cylinder base.

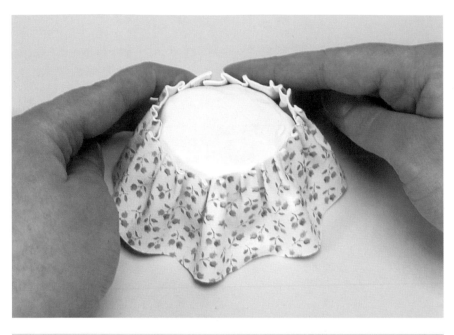

Gather the fabric piece, making tiny folds along the top of it. The clay will hold the gathers when pressed up against the raw clay on the cylinder.

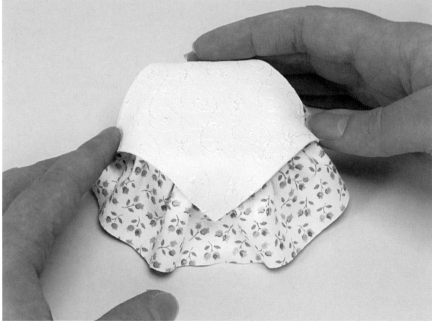

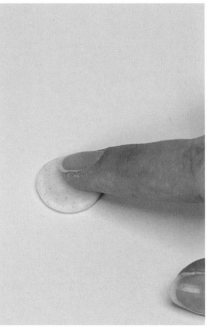

Step 3. Table Cloth. Make the top tablecloth the same way as the skirt, but use a lace material instead. Cut a 3" (7.6cm) square. Lay the square on the top and arrange it the way you like, keeping in mind where the back of the piece is (where the two ends of the skirt meet). You may need to glue the points of the square to the fabric with a little white glue to help hold them down.

Step 4. Teacups. Make the saucer from transparent clay tinted with green sand. Roll a $^7/_{16}$" (1.1cm) ball and flatten it into a $^{13}/_{16}$" (2.1cm) circle.

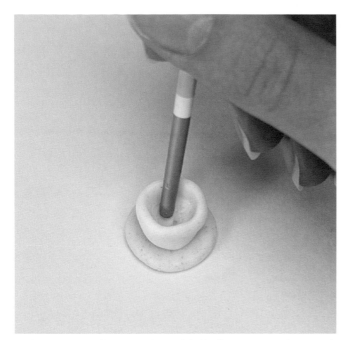

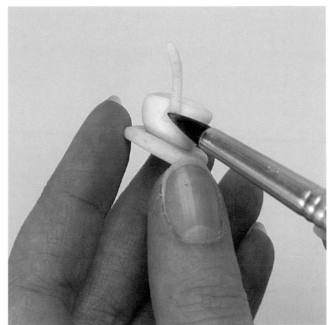

Make the teacup from a ½" (1.3cm) ball of transparent clay tinted with rose sand. Place the ball in the center of the saucer and use the end of a paintbrush to indent the center of the cup and secure it to the saucer.

Tip   Sometimes it is easier to pick up a piece if you work on a note card.

Make the handle from a ¼" (6.4mm) transparent ball tinted with green sand formed into a rope approximately 1" (2.5cm) long. With the blending tool, attach one end of the rope onto the cup with the rest of the rope pointing up.

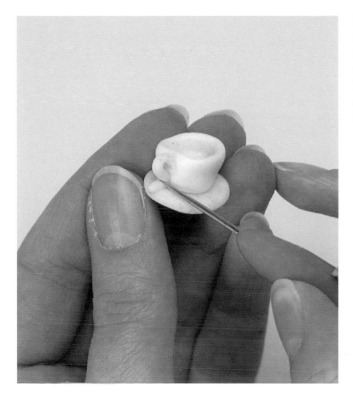

Bend the handle down and use the wide needle tool to press this end of the clay into the cup. Make two of these teacups and saucers. Add faces to both teacups. Have the handles on opposite sides so that each faces out when the teacups are glued to the table after being baked.

Step 5. Teapot. Make the teapot body from a ⅞" (2.2cm) transparent ball tinted with rose sand. Set the ball on the table and pinch the sides a little. This will give you a flat surface to put the face on later.

Make the top of the pot from a ⅞" (2.2cm) ball of clay tinted with rose sand. Place it on the top of the teapot and flatten it a little with your finger.

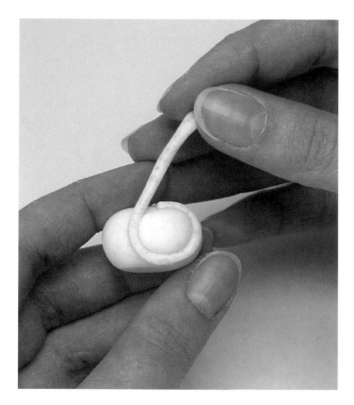

Make the rim on the top from a ⅜" (.95cm) ball of transparent clay tinted with green sand and roll into a rope ⅛" (.32cm) thick. Starting in the back, wrap the rope all the way around the lid. Add a small ball of clay to the top of the lid for a handle.

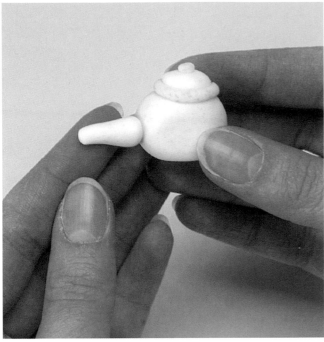

Make the spout from a ⁷⁄₁₆" (1.1cm) ball of transparent clay tinted with rose sand. Form into a skinny teardrop. Place the wide end of the teardrop against the side of the teapot.

Bend the spout upward and in toward the teapot. You will basically make a backward **S** shape with the clay.

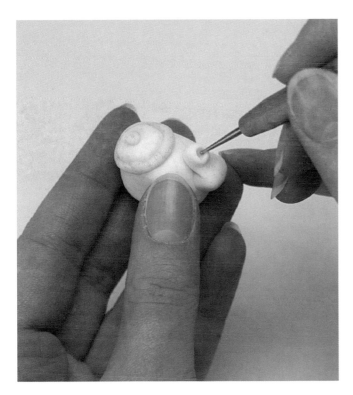

Step 6. Finishing Touches. In the very end of the spout, use the stylus to make a small indentation. Add the face to the teapot. Bake the teacups, teapot, and the table separately on the baking tray. After they have all cooled, paint and seal the eyes, and glue the teacups and teapot to the top of the table.

MARINA   TWIT & TWEET   BANG & BOOM   MS. DOT

RAY

summer

What better time than summer to look for natural elements from outside to add to your creations? A hike into the woods can become a shopping trip through nature. Especially if you live in a four-season climate, look for things that you might want to use during winter when the ground will be snow covered and things won't be so easy to find.

Ms. Dot

This leaf cane is one of my personal favorites. You can
achieve satisfying results
the first time you try it.
Thanks for this cane goes
out to Judith Skinner for
the Skinner Blend and to
Karen Lewis and Marie Segal
who developed the cane. If you
are anything like me, you will be
finding lots of things to add
leaves to!

SUPPLIES
- *clay colors:* red, black,
  green, white, pink,
  golden yellow
- basic tools (page 9)
- red wire

Step 1. Skinner Blend. Begin with a Skinner Blend of green to golden yellow, using half a block of each color.

Step 2. Clay Rollup. Run the sheet of clay through the no. 5 setting on a pasta machine. Cut off the solid yellow end. Starting at the lighter green end, begin to roll up the Skinner Blend into a bull's eye cane.

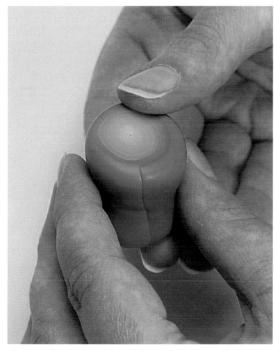

This is what it should look like when it is rolled up. For a little wider cane, pinch the ends in slightly to make it a little more stocky.

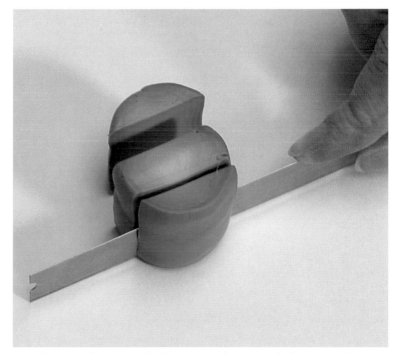

Step 3. Cane Division. With the cane standing on end, slice it into three equal pieces. Leave them standing together.

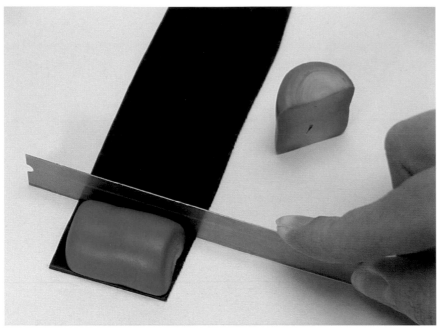

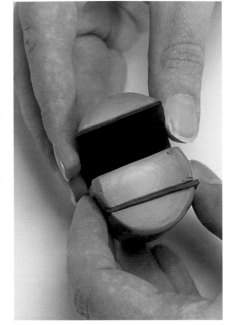

Step 4. Leaf Veins. Roll a sheet of black clay through the pasta machine on the no. 5 setting. Lay the first end piece on the black sheet with the flat side down, and trim the black clay to fit. Do the same with the other end piece.

Put the three pieces of the cane back together. There should be a black sheet between each piece.

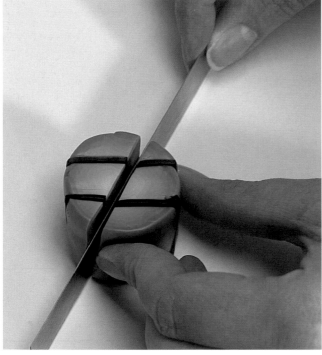

Make a diagonal cut across the cane.

This is where the magic happens. Flip one half of the cane upside down and put it back together with the remaining half. You should now be able to see the vein pattern on the leaf.

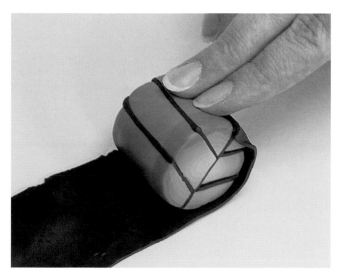

Wrap the cane in a black sheet of clay put through the pasta machine on the no. 5 setting.

Step 5. Cane Reduction. Lay the cane down and divide it in half. Reduce half of it, and leave the other half a larger size for now.

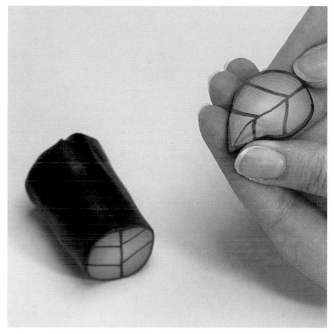

Step 6. Slice. Cut a slice ⅛" (.32cm) thick from the larger cane. Pinch the tip of it to create a leaf shape. Do not pinch the whole cane because it will need to be reduced and used for the next project (Twit & Tweet on page 83).

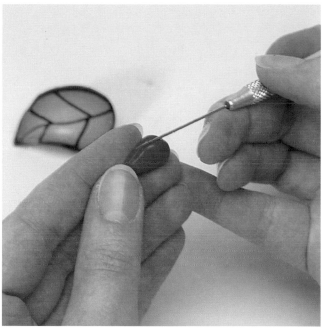

Step 7. Ladybug. To make the ladybug, begin with a ⅜" (.95cm) red ball formed into a teardrop. Lay the teardrop on its side and indent a line with the needle tool near the top for her wings.

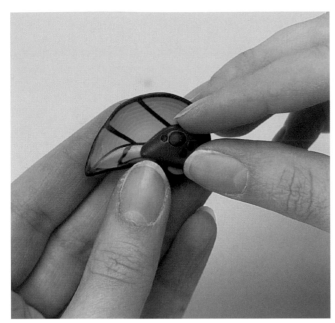

Place a few random black dots onto the wings. Place her on the leaf slice and fold the bottom edge of the leaf up to her.

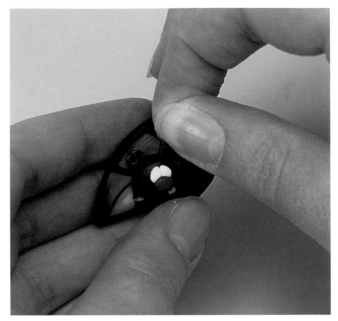

Make her head from a 5/16" (8cm) ball of black clay. Gently push her head onto her body and the leaf. Add her face. Use red wire for her antennas. Cut two 3/8" (.95cm) pieces of wire and curl the top ends to make the antennas. Push them into the top of her head. Either glue them in now or pull them out after baking and glue them in then.

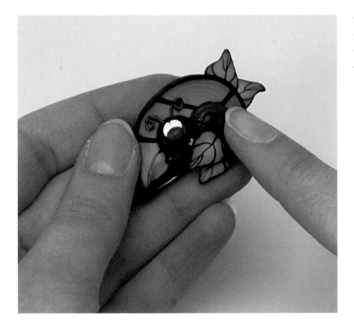

Step 8. Finishing Touches. Cut five slices from the smaller canes. Add two slices to the top corner and three to the bottom where the leaf is curled up. Then bake.

Twit & Tweet

The idea for this project was inspired by my parents. My dad creates three-dimensional frames to be used for keepsakes, then my mom designs and arranges people's personal items on the inside. I could not help but imagine different polymer clay scenes in these great frames. It is another way to display your polymer clay creations.

When you are planning your three-dimensional picture, make a rough drawing of your idea. This will help you figure out how to layer pieces. Creating something in the foreground on the glass adds to the three-dimensional effect. There are also molds that will give you a dimensional piece with a flat back, suitable for making these pictures. The possibilities for these frame projects are virtually endless. Ideas include seasons, special occasions, such as weddings or births, or even objects to match your home decor. The frames are available in a range of sizes to suit your needs.

SUPPLIES

- *clay colors:* pink, light blue, sky blue, FIMO Soft Raspberry, white, light brown, dark brown
- basic tools (page 9)
- leaf cane (from the Ms. Dot project)
- 3-D wood frame
- clay gun
- clay gun extruder (optional)

Step 1. Background Preparation. Begin by taking the frame apart. Lift the framing staples carefully and lift out the back and the glass. Work on the back of the frame first. Squeeze some white glue on the inside of the frame back. Smear it all over the back until a thin film of glue covers the entire side. Let the glue dry.

Step 2. First Layer. Make a Skinner Blend from sky blue to FIMO Soft Raspberry using a 2-ounce (56.7g) block of each color. Lay the glue side down onto the sheet of clay. Trim the blended sheet of clay to fit on the frame back.

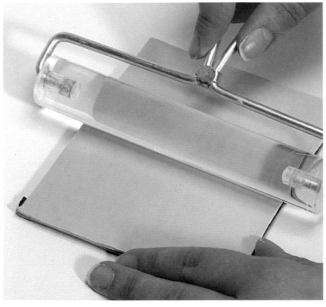

Lay the sheet on top of the glue-covered frame back and roll over it with a brayer to secure it to the glue and remove any air bubbles.

Step 3. Mold. To make the bark on the clay tree seem more realistic, make a mold from a real piece of bark. You can use scrap clay to make the mold. Lightly dust the scrap clay with baby powder so it does not stick to the bark, and press the bark into the raw piece of clay.

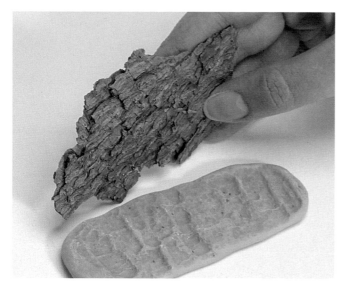

When you lift up the bark, the impression will be in the clay. Bake the mold and let it cool.

Step 4. Tree. Lightly dust the mold with baby powder. Marble together a 1⅜" (3.5cm) light brown ball and a 1" (2.5cm) dark brown ball, until there are very fine streaks in the clay. Press half of the marbled brown clay into the bark mold.

Lay the first piece of the tree on the side. Notice I left a space at the top and the bottom of the tree. This is so that when the backing is put back on the frame, it can still lay flat on the ledge. With the other half of the marbled brown clay, make a large branch and push it into the bark mold. Place the branch so that when the birds are put on it, they will be centered in the frame.

Step 5. Birds. The boy bluebird's body is a ½" (1.3cm) light blue ball formed into a fat teardrop. Make the white part of his chest from a ½" (1.3cm) white ball formed into a teardrop and flattened. Use your needle tool to indent two lines on each side of the teardrop.

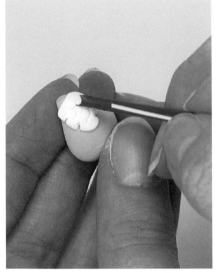

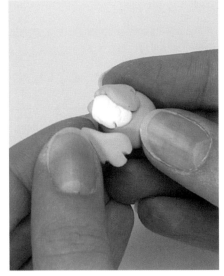

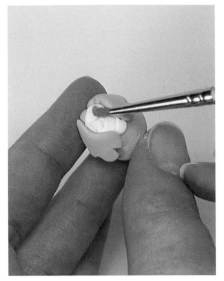

Place the white piece onto his body. To make a few scalloped impressions to simulate feathers, use a cut straw tool (instructions on page 101).

Make each wing from a ¼" (.64cm) light blue ball formed into a teardrop and flattened. With the needle tool, indent a few lines to the side of the teardrop to shape his wing. The tip of the teardrop should point to his back and the rounded end should be in the front.

Add just a touch of pink chalk or blush makeup to his chest.

Place the bluebird on the tree branch so that he is just above it. Make his head from a ⅜" (.95cm) light blue ball formed into a slightly flattened cone. Add a few little pieces of light blue clay to the top of his head for "hair." Make the girl bird in the same way. Add a bow to her head. Add their eyes and beaks. (See instructions for beaks on pages 58–59).

Step 6. Nest. Roll a 1" (2.5cm) light brown ball into a log and insert it into the clay gun and slowly squeeze the clay out. Use the disk that has seven holes in it.

To make the nest, fold in half the ropes that were made from the clay gun and twist them.

Finish twisting the ropes until they are about 2½" (6.4cm) long.

Attach the nest to the bottom part of the birds and part of the branch. Add a few leaves to the background and to the end of the branch.

Step 7. Leaves. Start by taking the glass front out of the frame.

Tip   If you cannot get the glass out and it is a wooden frame, you can just work from the inside of the frame. With this project we are trying to make it seem as though we are peeking through the leaves on the tree to see the bluebirds. Make several slices from the reduced leaf cane, scatter them around three sides of the glass and push them gently onto the glass. Flip the glass over once in a while to see how it will look from the front.

Hold the frame over the birds to make sure that everything you want to see is visible. Finish filling in the three sides with more leaves.

This is a view from the front; it is ready to put in the oven with the background piece. Bake the front of the frame with the glass side down, not the leaf side down.

Step 8. Assemble. After the leaves and the bluebirds have been baked and cooled, place the glass piece in first with the glass on the outside and the leaves on the inside.

Push the framing staples back down with the wide end of the stylus or the end of a paintbrush—not a sharp object.

Next, place the bluebirds in the frame and close the framing staples.

Bang & Boom

There are two different types of metallic clay: one containing mica and one containing glitter. The FIMO Soft metallic clays are transparent clays that have colored glitter in them. The colors include silver, gold, black, red, green and blue. The other kind of metallic clay contains small particles of mica that reflects light. PREMO! Sculpey metallic colors are gold, silver, copper, red, green, blue and pearl. FIMO Classic also carries a pearl white with mica particles. A wide range of metallic colors can be made by mixing metallic colors with other metallic colors or with nonmetallic colors.

SUPPLIES
- *clay colors:* metallic blue, metallic red, metallic silver, yellow, orange
- basic tools (page 9)
- red wire
- mini star cutter
- medium star cutter

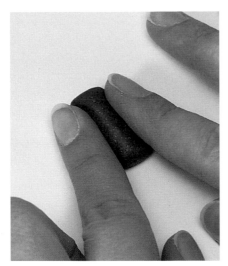

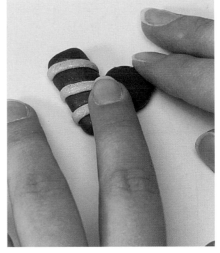

Step 1. Blue Firecracker. Roll a ⅝" (1.6cm) metallic blue ball into a 1⅛" (3cm) long log. Lay the log on the table and gently press the sides down a little to make the back flat but maintain the roundness on the front.

Make a ⅛" (.32cm) wide silver rope and wrap it three times around the front side of the blue piece. Use your finger to flatten the silver rope onto the blue cylinder.

Step 2. Red Firecracker. Make a ¼" (.64cm) metallic red ball. Lay it next to the blue firecracker, slightly overlapping it, and press down with your fingers on the sides, making the back flat.

Use a ³⁄₁₆" (.48cm) star cutter to cut out blue and silver stars to add to the bottom of the red firecracker. Alternate colors along the bottom.

Step 3. Faces. Add faces to both of the firecrackers. Put a red nose on the blue firecracker, and a blue nose on the red one. Use a ³⁄₈" (.48cm) star cutter to cut out two yellow stars and a ⁵⁄₁₆" (0.8cm) star cutter to cut out two orange stars. Also cut two ¼" (1.9cm) lengths of red wire. Sandwich each wire between a yellow and orange star and insert the wires into the top of each firecracker.

Ray

This beautiful cane was developed by Donna Kato. She created this type of cane using transparent clay and imitation metal leaf. For some interesting effects you can also try this technique with plain transparent clay and leaf, adding the thin slices to a colored background.

I have found that making my own templates can be very useful, especially if I cannot find a cookie cutter in the shape that I want. You can make a template out of pretty much anything, but I find that they last longer if made from posterboard and laminated as follows:

1. Draw or trace the design on posterboard.
2. Trim around the edge of your designs but not on the cutting line.
3. Next, laminate it with self-adhesive laminating sheets or a laminating machine. You will get the most from a laminating sheet if you laminate more than one design at a time.
4. After both sides of the posterboard are laminated, finish cutting out your design, this time on the line.

To use the template, place it on a sheet of clay and use a ceramic scalpel or thin craft knife to trace around the design. For the best results, move the knife in a continuous motion until the design is completely cut out.

SUPPLIES
- *clay colors:* transparent yellow, transparent orange, white, pink
- gold leaf

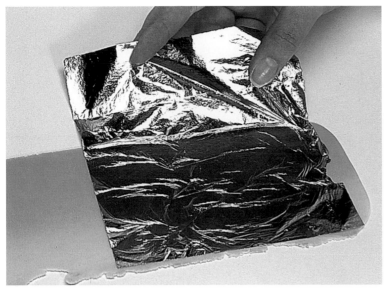

Step 1. Preparation. Make a Skinner Blend with a 2-ounce (56.7g) block each of yellow and orange transparent clay. Run through a pasta machine on the no. 4 setting. Place a piece or two of imitation gold leaf on the sheet of clay and gently pat down the leaf so that it sticks to the clay.

Tightly roll the sheet of clay and the gold leaf together.

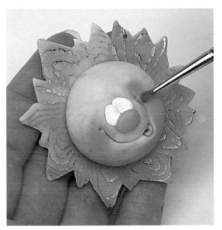

Use a new NuBlade to make steep slices from the cane. Make them as thin as possible.

Step 2. Sun Rays. Cut out a sun shape from transparent yellow clay that has been run through the no. 1 setting on the pasta machine. Begin laying cane slices all over the top of the sun rays. When the piece is covered, lay a piece of tissue paper over the rays and burnish the surface until it is flat and even. For a photo reference of this step, see the heart pin on page 39. (Note: If you'd like to create a pattern for this project, trace around the picture of Ray on page 92 and size it to your liking.)

Step 3. Face. Make a ⅞" (2.2cm) ball of marbled transparent yellow and orange. Place it in the center of the sun rays and gently press down on the sides of the ball. Add his face and brush blush onto his cheeks.

Marina

In my opinion, polymer clay and snow globes were meant to go together. Just think of how many different things you can make with the snow globes alone. Not only can you design the object to go into the globe, but you can also create very interesting bases for the globe as well, either painted or covered with clay.

The snow globe can be filled with a water mixture, allowing snow to fall around an object, but it can also be a creative display container for pieces as well. Snow globes are available in many sizes. You can also purchase windup music boxes to insert into the bottom of the wooden base.

If you should decide to fill the snow globe, mix equal parts of distilled water and glycerin. When you add either synthetic snowflakes or glitter, a little goes a long way. You will need much less than you might think. Also, when you design the object to put in water, remember that it will be magnified in the filled globe.

When you glue the base of the globe onto the rubber stopper, glue only around the middle. The edges of the rubber stopper need to be able to flex and bend to achieve a tight seal when the base is inserted into the globe.

SUPPLIES
- *clay colors:* FIMO Classic Champagne, flesh, tan, metallic blue, FIMO Soft Brilliant Blue, metallic green, FIMO Soft Lime Green, FIMO Soft Tropical Green, transparent green, light yellow, white, turquoise, pink, FIMO Soft Rose Quartz
- basic tools (page 9)
- 4" (10cm) snow globe
- shell
- black seed beads
- distilled water and glycerin
- coffee stir

Step 1. Base. To create the base, marble together a ⅞" (2.2cm) Champagne ball and a ⅞" (2.2cm) tan ball. Flatten the clay into a 2½" (6.4cm) diameter circle. Make sure that it fits on the gray stopper for the snow globe. Pounce a toothbrush on the base to create sand texture.

Step 2. Shell. Use a 2" (5cm) diameter shell. Place a 1" (2.5cm) ball of Champagne or light colored scrap clay on the inside of the shell.

Place the shell, with the ball of clay under it, on top of the sand base and press down. This should press the clay ball into the sand base.

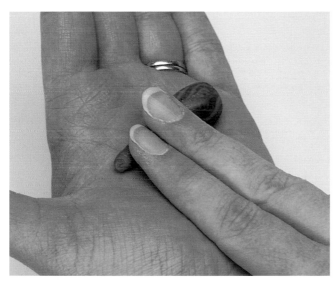

Step 3. Lower Body. Make the mermaid's lower body from mixing a ¾" (1.9cm) metallic blue ball with a ¾" (1.9cm) metallic green ball. Form the clay into a tapered cone shape.

Pull the narrow end of the cone over to the side and twist it a little.

Place the lower half of her body on the top of the shell. Arrange the tip of the cone (her body) off to the side of the shell. Use the handle of the wide stylus or another rounded, blunt-end tool to make an indentation in the top of the cone. This is where the top half of her body will be placed.

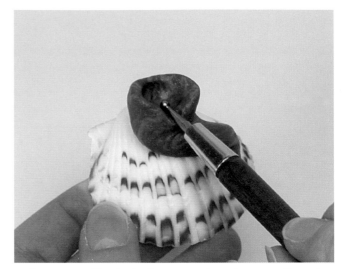

In the portion of her body shown, use the stylus or needle tool to make a **V** shaped impression.

Step 4. Top Half of Body. Make the top of her body from a ¾" (1.9cm) clay ball. Form it into a teardrop and then twist a small portion down from the wide end to fit into the lower-half of her body. Insert the wide end of the top half into the indentation in the lower half.

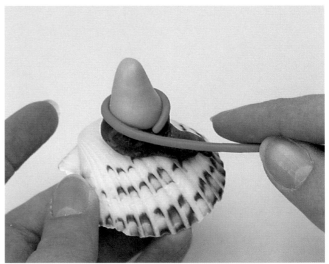

Make a ⅛" (.32cm) wide rope of transparent green clay. Wrap it around her body where the upper and lower halves meet. Make sure to re-create the **V** in the front.

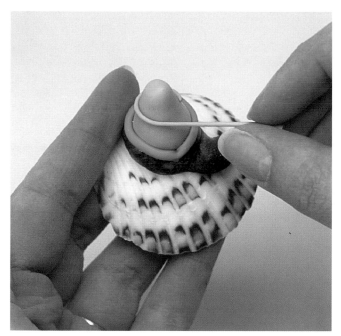

Make a ¹⁄₁₆" (.16cm) wide pink rope and wrap it around her body ¼" (.64cm) down from the top.

Make each shell from a ³⁄₁₆" (.48cm) pink ball. Flatten each one to a ⁵⁄₁₆" (0.8cm) circle. Use the needle tool to make the shell indentations on each. Place them next to each other on top of the pink rope on her body.

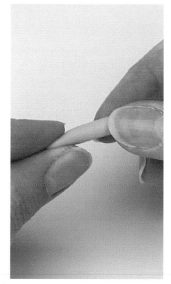

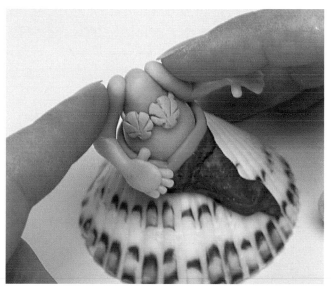

Step 5. Arms and Hands.
Make each arm from a ⁷⁄₁₆" (1.1cm) clay ball. Roll the ball into a 1¼" (3.2cm) long log. Flatten ¼" (.64cm) of the bottom of the log for the hand.

The top view of the log should look like this.

Attach both arms to her body.

Step 6. Head. Make her head from a ¼" (1.9cm) clay ball. Attach her head to her body and add her face and ears. Instead of making a smile, create a teardrop opening for her mouth using the needle tool. Use a small black holeless bead for each eye.

Step 7. Hair. Her hair is made from an ¹¹⁄₁₆" (1.7cm) light yellow ball. Flatten it to ⅛" (.32cm) thick and form into an oval with a small indentation off to one side. This will be the part in her bangs.

Place the hair piece on her head and form it to your liking.

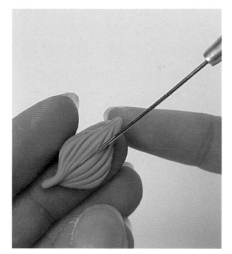

Step 8. Fins. Make each fin from a ³⁄₈"
(.95cm) transparent green ball. Shape each
ball into a flattened teardrop, ¹⁄₁₆" to ¹⁄₈"
(.16cm to .32cm) thick, and create the
lines using the needle tool. Make two fins.

Attach the fins with the blending tool.
Press the underside of the wide end of the
fin to the edge of her body with the blending tool. Then bend the fin down to cover
where the underside is attached.

Arrange the fins in a pleasing fashion.

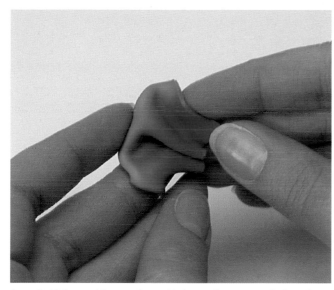

Step 9. Fish. Marble together a ½" (1.3cm) turquoise ball and a
½" (1.3cm) Brilliant Blue ball. An alternative is to use a leftover
piece from the Skinner Blend that was made to cover the base.
Roll the clay out and make a few folds in it.

Place the clay at the top center of the globe. Press this "wave"
onto the glass, forming it to the contours of the globe. Arrange it
the way you like.

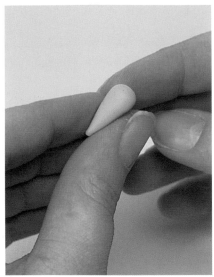

Make the fish from a ⁷⁄₁₆" (1.1cm) Lime Green ball. Roll into a teardrop.

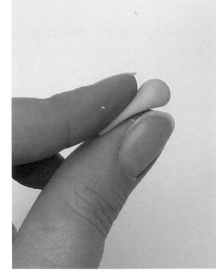

Flatten all of the teardrop but the wide end, which will become his head.

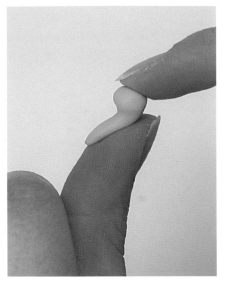

Roll his head forward to create definition between his head and body. This picture is a side view.

Place the fish leaning against the wave. His head will face the front, and his body will be off to the side.

Make each of the top fins on the fish from a ³⁄₁₆" (.48cm) Tropical Green and Lime Green marbled ball. Shape them the same way that you made the mermaid's fins. Attach them on either side of his body with the blending tool.

Make each of the bottom fins from a ¼" (.64cm) Tropical Green and Lime Green marbled ball. Shape and attach in the same way as the mermaid's fins.

His eyes are each a ⅛" (.32cm) white ball. Attach them to the top of his head. Press in a holeless black bead for each eye.

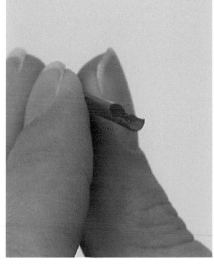

Using the needle tool, create his smile and add his tongue.

Make the cut straw tool from a small coffee stir. Use a small pair of scissors or a craft knife to cut away half of the straw opening. This will create a U shape perfect for making small scales.

Use the cut straw tool to make scales on the fish's body.

Step 10. Base Decoration. Make a Skinner Blend from turquoise to Brilliant Blue clay. Run the sheet of clay through the no. 5 setting on the pasta machine. Cover the wooden base with a thin layer of glue and let dry. Wrap the Skinner Blend around the wooden base; do not trap any air bubbles. Bake it by itself.

Step 11. Coral. After the base has cooled, begin adding the coral pieces. I made the coral from flattened teardrops of Rose Quartz clay. After making the teardrops, arrange them using the pictures as a guide. Once you decide where you want to place them, lift each piece slightly and add a very small dab of glue underneath.

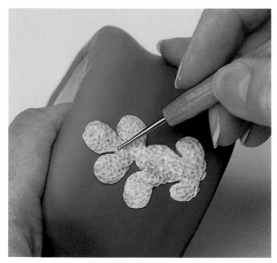

To give the coral texture, use the wide end of the stylus and make impressions all over the coral piece.

Step 12. Sand. Make the band of sand that goes along the bottom of the base from a ³⁄₁₆" (4.8cm) wide and 13½" (34cm) long rope of marbled Champagne and tan clay. Flatten the entire rope with your finger or a roller until it is about ¼" wide (.64cm). Use an old toothbrush to make the sand texture in the clay.

Add a dab of glue to the bottom edge. Begin wrapping the sand edge along the bottom of the base. Add small amounts of glue as you go along. With your finger or blending tool, blend the point where the rope ends meet. Use the toothbrush again to go over the blended seam.

Step 13. Fish. The fish are simple shapes with eyes and fins. Use scrap pieces of bright, tropical colors to create the fish. Make them flat, and use a dab of glue to secure them to the base. Make the eyes and fins the same way as the mermaid's, but smaller.

Step 14. Assemble. Bake the base, the mermaid on the shell and the sand base. Once the clay pieces have cooled, glue the mermaid to the shell and the shell to the sand base. It is important to use silicone glue if your globe will be filled with water. Make sure to realign any impressions you may have made in the sand when you pressed the shell into it in the beginning.

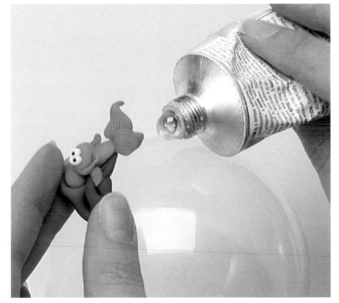

Next, after the shell and sand base have dried completely, glue the bottom of the sand base to the rubber stopper. It is important that the edges of the sand and the stopper are aligned. Glue the fish to the top center of the glass globe. After the glue has dried on all pieces, assemble the snow globe. If you wish to fill the water globe, first insert the rubber stopper. Then pull back an edge of the stopper and fill with a water and glycerin mixture. Sprinkle in a little snow or glitter when the globe is half full and then finish filling. Attach the globe to the base.

AUTUMN PAIGE   FRANKIE   CELESTE GOBBLES

NUTTY

autumn

Autumn to me is one of the most beautiful times of year. The contrast of the golden colors against a blue sky can make even the most brisk days feel warm. I hope these projects can warm your heart as you learn a few techniques such as making an ikat cane, making hair and using colored powders with your clay.

Nutty

SUPPLIES
- *clay colors:* FIMO Classic Golden Yellow, FIMO Classic Ochre, orange, red, tan, brown, white, pink
- basic tools (page 9)
- cotton swab
- gold and copper Pearl Ex

Powders, from matte chalks to metallic powders, can add visual interest to a project. They can be used as an accent or to cover something entirely. A few different types of powders you can use include

- Pearl Ex
- eye shadow
- blush
- pastels
- chalks

I have also found a wealth of different powdered colors in makeup departments. Eye shadows and blush are available in matte or pearl colors. Use brown eye shadow around the edge of a faux cookie to make it look more real.

The powders adhere best to raw (unbaked) clay. They can be applied with a fingertip, a small or large brush, cotton swabs or makeup sponges/applicators. It takes only a sparse amount of powder to cover or accent a piece. Be sure to tap any excess powder off of the application tool before applying. An easy way to get only a little on your finger (or applicator) is to slowly turn the container upside down (with the cap on), turn it back over, let it sit for about thirty seconds to let the powder settle and then open it. Next, dab the applicator on the inside of the top of the container. Tipping it upside down allows a thin film to stick to the top. A piece that powder has been applied to should be sealed with a matte or gloss sealer after it is baked.

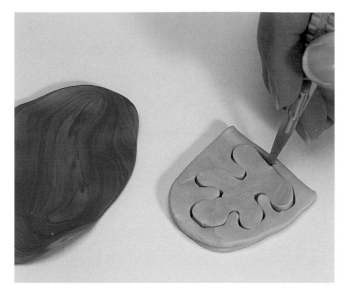

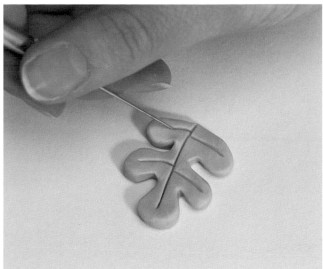

Step 1. Leaves. Marble together red, Golden Yellow and orange. Marble together a separate piece of Golden Yellow and Ochre clay. Flatten each marbled piece by putting it through the pasta machine on the no. 2 setting. Fold it in half to create a double thickness. Cut a leaf out of each of the marbled colors. Smooth the edges of each leaf.

Use the needle tool to indent veins on each leaf.

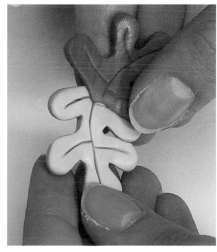

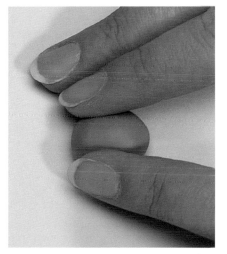

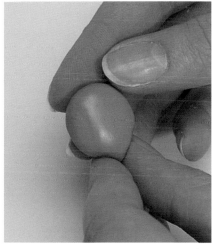

Step 2. Put Leaves Together. Join the wide end of each leaf together overlapping them a little. Slightly angle the orange leaf down.

Step 3. Acorn. Make the acorn from a ¾" (2cm) tan ball. Lay the ball down on the table and gently press the sides down to give it a flat back.

Pick up the acorn and pinch the very tip of one end.

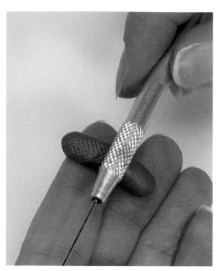

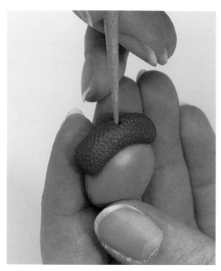

Make the cap of the acorn from a ½" (1.3cm) brown ball formed into a log. Use the pattern on the handle of the needle tool to impress the cap for texture. Roll it back and forth until the top and sides are covered.

Press the cap of the acorn onto the top of the acorn. Use a pointed tool to make a small indent in the top of the acorn cap for the stem.

The stem is a ³⁄₁₆" (4.8cm) brown ball formed into a teardrop. Put the small end into the hole in the top of the acorn cap, and bend the rest forward.

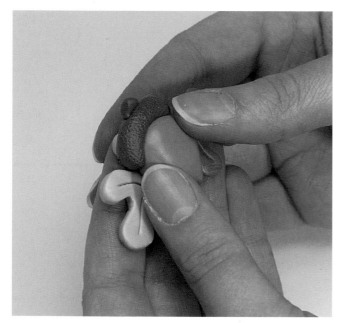

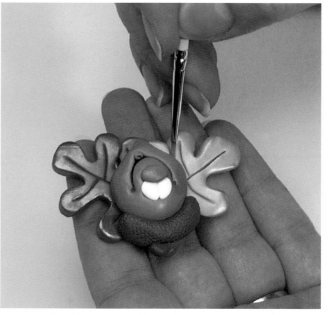

Gently press the acorn onto the leaves. Then add the face.

Use a tiny brush to apply gold powder to the yellow leaf edges and copper powder to the the orange leaf edges to accent them.

Autumn Paige

This cane creates zigzag patterns that resemble the markings on a striped cat and is referred to as an Ikat cane. This cane was created and developed by Donna Kato. It can be used on more than just animals, although it does add a great detail to them. When you apply slices of this cane to an animal figure, consider the direction that the stripes would naturally go. This will help to add more character to your finished piece. Also experiment with different colors and combinations.

You can create the sweater look by simply adding any colored clay to FIMO Soft Stone Jasper clay. The tiny brown fibers in stone effects clay make it resemble a knit material.

SUPPLIES
- *clay colors:* red, yellow, FIMO Classic Ochre, FIMO Soft Stone Jasper, orange, pink, white, FIMO Classic Champagne
- basic tools (page 9)
- white or ivory wire

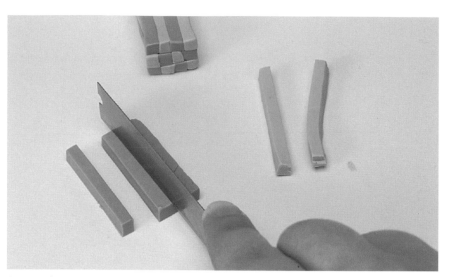

Step 1. Ikat Cane. Create a checkerboard cane. To make a checkered pattern, run a 1" (2.5cm) ball of Ochre through the pasta machine on the no. 1 setting. Fold it in half to double its thickness. Make a few slices (refer to photo). Do the same with a 1" (2.5cm) Champagne ball. Alternate the colors, making a block four slices across and three high.

This is what the checkerboard should look like.

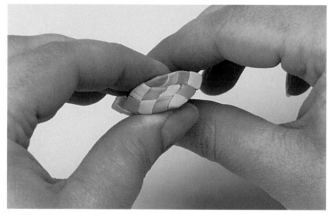

Hold the square at an angle so it looks like a diamond shape. Flatten the points of the diamond toward the center. Run through the pasta machine on the no. 1 setting.

Fold in half and run through the pasta machine again. Repeat this three to four times. After the end has a good pattern, cut into four pieces and stack them on top of each other. You need to cut the end to see the pattern, which should be a zigzag pattern of the two different colors.

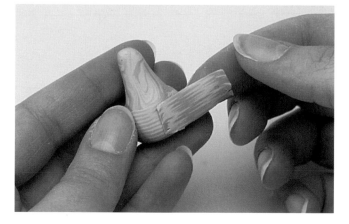

Step 2. Cat's Body. Make the cat's body from a ¾" (1.9cm) ochre and Champagne marbled clay ball. Cover the bottom half of her body with thin slices from the ikat cane. Note the direction of the stripes. You don't need to cover the top; it will be covered by her sweater.

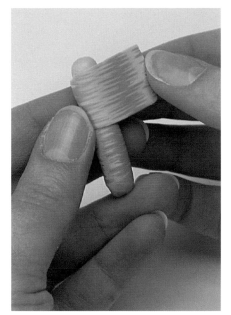

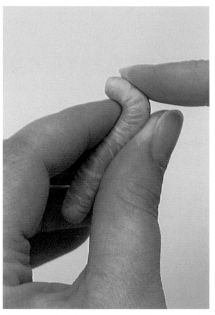

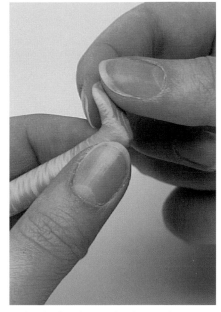

Step 3. Hind Legs and Feet. For each leg, roll a ½" (1.3cm) Ochre and Champagne marbled clay ball into a 1¼" (3.2cm) log. The legs are a little thin because you will be adding clay around each leg. Cover with thin slices of the cane. Make two hind legs.

Shape the foot by bending ½" (1.3cm) of the end of the log into an L shape.

Make the foot longer for the cat than you would for a human, so that you can create her paw. Pinch the top so that it is approximately ⅝" (1.6cm) from the top of her foot to the bottom of her heel. The top should be thinner than the bottom.

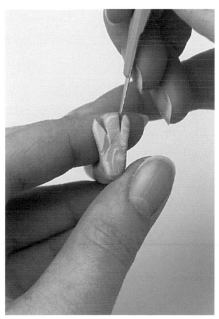

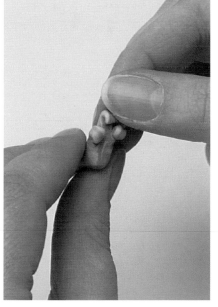

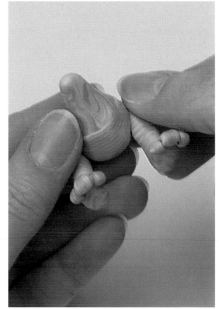

Use a scalpel or knife to make two cuts for her toes. Hold the piece on your finger to cut only if the blade that you are using is very dull. If the blade is sharp, set the piece on the edge of the table to cut it. The toe in the middle should be a little larger than the two on either side.

Roll the two side toe pieces down and then roll the middle one down.

Cut the end of each leg at a 45° angle and attach them to the body.

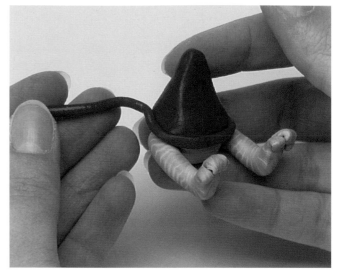

Step 4. Sweater. To make the sweater, roll a ⅝" (1.6cm) ball of mixed red and Jasper clay. Form it into a teardrop and then insert a pointed tool into the wide end. Roll it back and forth until the inside of the sweater is a hollow cone.

Place the sweater (cone) on the cat's body. Roll a ⅛" (3.2mm) wide red rope and wrap it around the bottom edge of the sweater.

Use the thin needle tool to indent lines all the way around the rope for the ribbing on the sweater.

Make each sleeve of the sweater from a ⅜" (.95cm) red clay ball. Form each ball into a log and make a small indent in the wide end for her paw. Set aside.

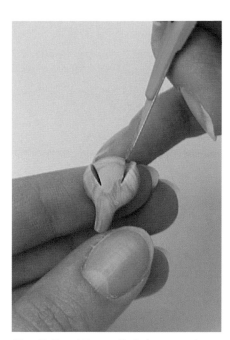  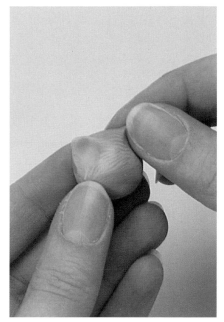

Step 5. Front Paws. Each front paw is a ¼" (.64cm) ball covered with slices from the cane. Flatten the ball and twist a small piece of the clay down to be put in the hole on the sleeve (refer to photo). Make two cuts in the paw the same way as for the feet.

Insert a paw into each sleeve, and attach both arms to the body at the same time. Arrange the arms so that she is leaning back on one and has the other paw facing up in the air.

Step 6. Head. To make her head, start with a ⅝" (1.6cm) Champagne clay ball and cover with cane slices. For her ears, pinch a very small amount of clay on each side of the top of the ball. Refer to picture.

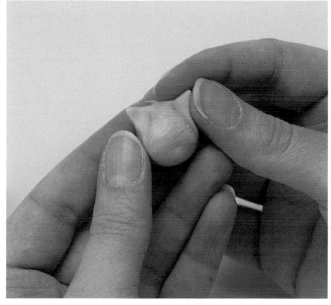 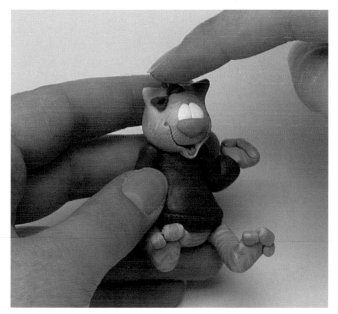

Further define her ears by pinching in the opposite direction just enough to point the ears.

Attach the head to her body and add her face. Position her head so that she is looking at her raised paw. Add a small red bow in front of her ear.

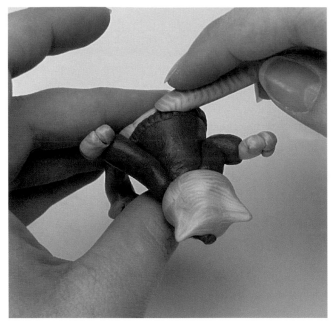

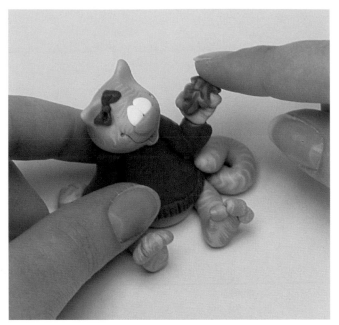

Step 7. Tail. Make the cat's tail from a ½" (1.3cm) ball rolled into a 2" (5cm) rope and cover it with the cane slices. Attach the tail in the middle of her body under the sweater line.

Step 8. Finishing Touches. Add to her paw a simple leaf made from marbling red, orange and yellow clay together.

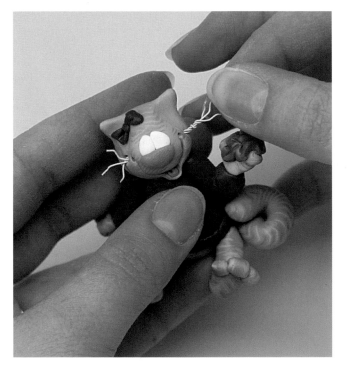

Make her whiskers from wire cut into ⅜" (.95cm) long pieces and twisted together. Push them into her head right next to her smile.

Frankie

Adding hair to a character can be a lot of fun and really bring out the personality of your creation. When you sculpt a head, think about how you want the hair to be. I often have found that if the hair does not look quite the way I expected it to, it was because the head was not the right shape. Remember to leave enough of a forehead for the character to accept hair. Many materials can be used to simulate hair. Here are just a few:

- yarn
- raffia
- ribbon
- mohair
- synthetic hair
- wigs
- human hair
- faux fur
- clay
- string
- embroidery floss
- strips of fabric
- silk flower petals
- paper twist

When you walk through a craft store, begin to look in new ways at the different materials you see.

SUPPLIES
- *clay colors:* green, purple, brown, black, pink, white
- basic tools (page 9)
- black yarn
- two ¼" (.64cm) gold screws

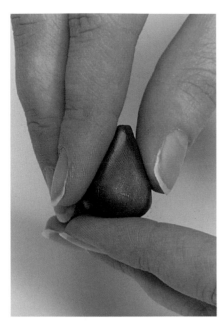

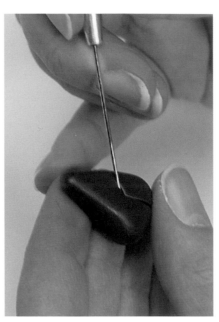

Step 1. Legs. Make Frankie's legs from an ¹¹⁄₁₆" (1.8cm) brown clay ball shaped into a cone and flattened slightly on the top and back.

Use the needle tool to make a line from the center of his pants down to create two pant legs. Then create a small **V** indentation at the top of the pant line.

Step 2. Shoes. Make each shoe from a ³⁄₈" (.95cm) black ball shaped into a teardrop. Flatten half of the teardrop, from the middle to the tip, using your fingers. Attach both feet to the bottom of his pants, with the flattened half of the teardrop under his pant legs.

Add a heel line to the bottom of each shoe with the needle tool.

Step 3. Shirt. Make Frankie's shirt from a ⁵⁄₈" (1.6cm) purple ball shaped into a cone. Insert the pointed tool into the wide end of his shirt and create an opening for the pants to go into.

Insert the tapered end of the pants into the wide end of the shirt. Gently pinch the top and back to secure the shirt to the pants.

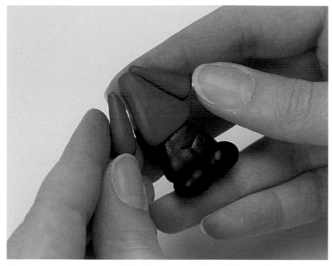

Make each arm from a ⅜" (.95cm) purple ball formed into a cone shape. Attach both arms to the body at the same time.

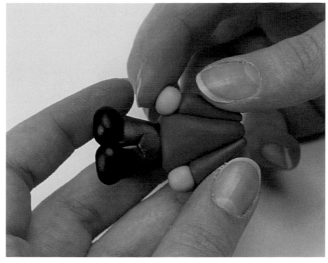

Make each hand from a ⁵⁄₁₆" (0.8cm) ball of green clay. Attach them beneath each sleeve.

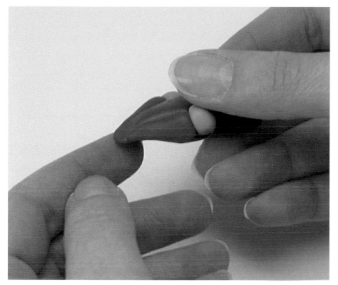

Step 4. Head. Flatten the top of his shirt a little so that his head has something more secure to rest on.

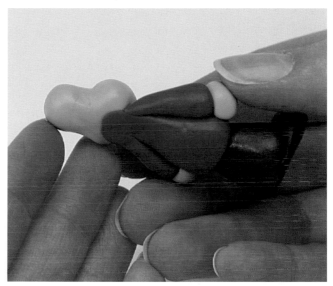

Shape his head from a ⅝" (1.6cm) green ball and attach it to his body, making sure that it overlaps onto his shirt.

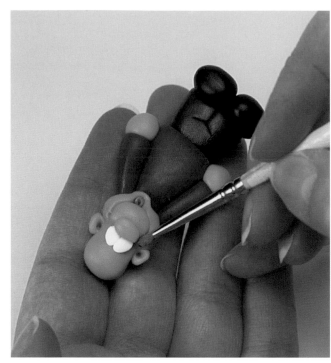

Add his face and apply blush to his cheeks.

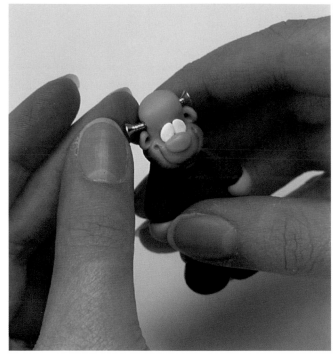

Step 5. Finishing Touches. Twist ¼" (.64cm) screws into either side of his head. He is ready to bake.

After he has baked and cooled, paint and seal his eyes. For his hair, cut ¾" (2cm) lengths of black yarn and glue them to the back of his head. After the glue has dried, trim the yarn so there is an even, straight hairline across the top.

Celeste

Many miniature accessories found in craft and hobby shops can be used with your characters. In fact, just looking at all of the miniature pieces in a store can inspire some great ideas for characters.

Most wood, glass and ceramic items can be baked with the piece. If you find a plastic item that you really want to use, I suggest that you form the piece around the object and then pull the object out before you bake the piece. After baking, you can glue the item back into its proper place.

Miniatures are a great way to accessorize your character without having to do all of the work, and they add more detail to a piece.

SUPPLIES
- *clay colors:* black, flesh, brown, gold, white, pink
- basic tools (page 9)
- miniature broom

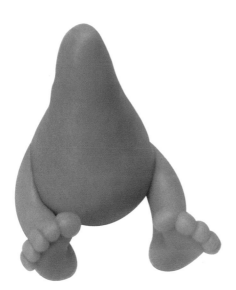

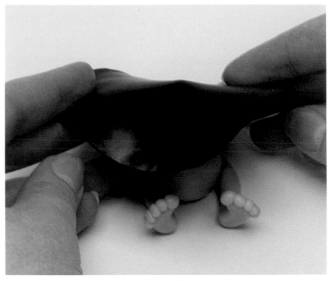

Step 1. Body. Make the body from a 1" (2.5cm) flesh clay ball. Make each leg/foot from a ⅝" (1.6cm) flesh clay ball.

Step 2. Gown. Run a black sheet of clay through the pasta machine on the no. 4 setting. Cut a 3½" (8.9cm) diameter circle of clay and drape it over her body.

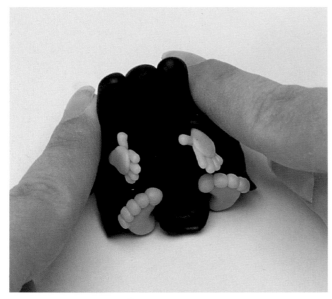

Make each sleeve from a ⅝" (1.6cm) black ball. Form each sleeve like the angel's sleeves on page 43. Attach a hand to each sleeve and put the sleeves on the body at the same time.

Step 3. Head and Hair. Make her head from a ¾" (2cm) flesh clay ball.

Add her face and ears. For her hair, start with the bangs. Roll a ¹⁄₁₆" (.16cm) wide brown rope and cut into ⅜" (.95cm) long pieces. Attach them to her forehead.

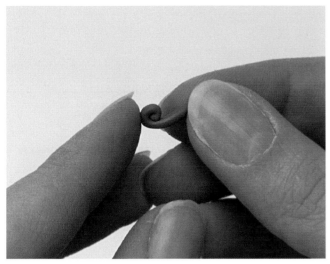

To make her pigtails, roll out a ¹⁄₁₆" (.16cm) wide brown clay rope. Cut 1" (2.5cm) long pieces. You will need about ten of them for each side. Curl only the end of each piece. Arrange ten pieces together for each side. Pinch them together enough to secure them to each other, but don't press them so hard that you lose the detail.

Attach a pigtail to each side of her head. The back of her head does not need hair because her hat will cover it.

Make her gold barrettes from a ¹⁄₁₆" (.16cm) wide gold clay rope. Wrap a small piece around each pigtail where it meets her head.

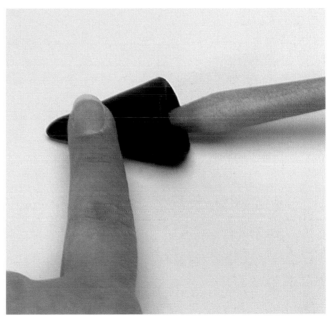

Step 4. Hat. Make the hat from a ¹³⁄₁₆" (2.1cm) black ball formed into a cone. Use the pointed tool to make a hollow cone by rolling the tool back and forth in the cone.

When the brim of the hat is as wide as you want it, place the hat on her head.

Arrange the top part of the hat. Add a gold buckle, and put a star at the top.

Step 5. Broom. Add the miniature broom to her hands. After you have figured out just how you want the broom positioned, add a dab of superglue to the underside of her hands and place them on the broom.

Gobbles

Several things can be created with flat-backed shapes. We have already discussed using them in three-dimensional frames, but you can also make magnets and buttons. Think about adjusting the size of the pins in this book to make magnets and buttons. Larger pieces may require two magnets to hold them up.

There are at least four ways to make buttons:

1. Glue a button shank to the back of a flat shape.
2. Create two or more button-holes that a needle can be threaded through.
3. Glue a button cover on the back of a baked piece.
4. Cover metal buttons with clay.

For inspiration for buttons, look in sewing stores. As long as your design is solid, put together well and not too fragile, you can machine wash them (as long as you use FIMO or Premo Sculpey!). Use cool/cold water and dry pieces at a low to medium temperature in the dryer. They should not be dry-cleaned.

SUPPLIES

- *clay colors:* light brown, brown, white, yellow, red
- basic tools (page 9)

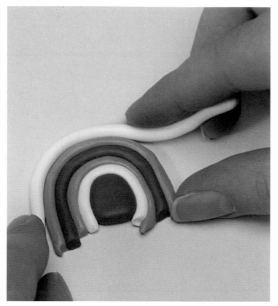

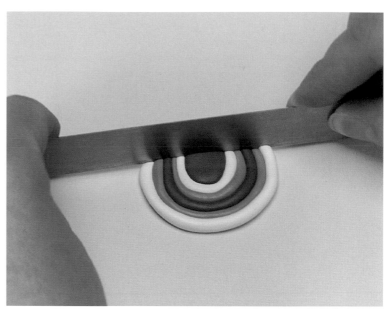

Step 1. Feathers. Start with a ⁷⁄₁₆" (1.1cm) brown ball flattened on your work surface. Then make ⅛" (.32cm) wide ropes out of white, light brown and brown clay. First wrap the white rope and the brown flattened ball, arching it like a rainbow. Then add light brown, brown and finish it with white.

Trim the bottom of the turkey feathers to create a straight edge.

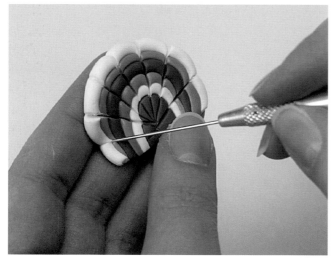

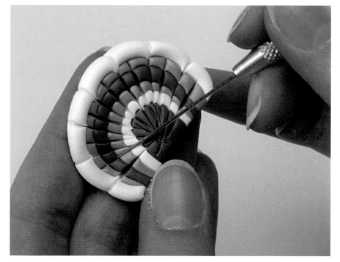

Use the needle tool and pull a line through to the brown center. Do this all the way around the feathers.

Add a line between your first lines, but start these at the light brown rope. This helps to give the illusion of feathers.

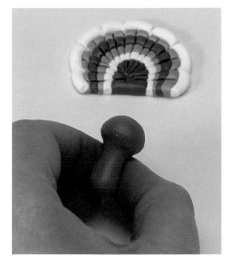

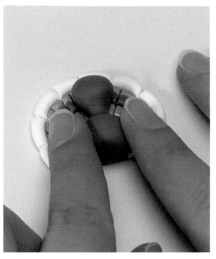

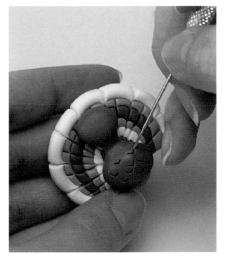

Step 2. Body. Make his body from a ⅝"
(1.6cm) brown ball. Roll into a log shape
and then about ½" (1.3cm) down from the
top, roll it between your fingers to create
the shape shown in the picture.

Lay the turkey down on the feathers and
gently press the sides of the turkey down
to adhere his body to the feathers.

Use the needle tool or a cut straw to make
crescent marks on his chest to simulate
feathers.

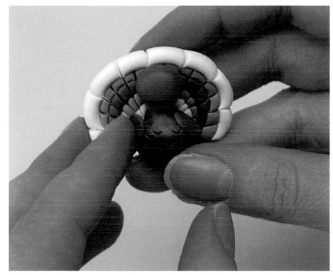

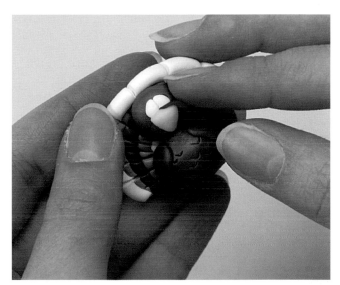

Make each wing from a ³⁄₁₆" (.48cm) brown ball shaped into a flat
teardrop. Attach to the sides of his body with the wide end of
each teardrop at the top.

Step 3. Face. Add his eyes. Make his beak from a ³⁄₁₆" (.48cm)
yellow ball formed into a triangle. Attach right below his eyes.
Make the red snood from a ⅛" (.32cm) red ball shaped into a
very tapered teardrop and add it to the top of his beak. Place the
point in the middle of the beak and hang the rest over the side.

resources

Polymer Clay

AMACO
(American Art Clay Co., Inc.)
4717 W. Sixteenth St.
Indianapolis, IN 46222
(800) 374-1600
www.amaco.com
Wholesale supplier of FIMO Classic, FIMO Soft, FIMO Glossy Lacquer and clay shapers.

Glass Attic (web site)
www.glassattic.com
This Web site is Diane Black's encyclopedia of information on polymer clay. The site contains nearly 500 pages of information relating to all aspects of polymer clay.

Polyform Products
1901 Estes Ave.
Elk Grove Village, IL 60007
(847) 427-0020
www.sculpey.com
Manufacturers of PREMO! Sculpey, Super Sculpey, Sculpey III and Flex molds.

Prairie Craft Company
P.O. Box 209
Florissant, CO 80816-0209
(800) 779-0615
www.prairiecraft.com
A source for PREMO! Sculpey, Super Sculpey, Sculpey III, Liquid Sculpey, Elasticlay, FIMO Classic and FIMO Soft. Also books, videos, tools and tips for the polymer clay artist.

Timothy and Stacey Morgan
P.O. Box 162
Owego, NY 13827
(607) 659-7755
E-mail: tmorgan1@twcny.rr.com
www.StaceyMorgan.com
A source for most of the items used in this book: clay sets for the different projects, tools, snow globes, pattern packets for clay, 3-D memory frames, molds. Also a limited number of finished pieces created by Stacey Morgan.

Wee Folk Creations
18476 Natchez Ave.
Prior Lake, MN 55372
www.weefolk.com
A source for PREMO! Sculpey, Super Sculpey, Sculpey III, Elasticlay, Cernit, FIMO Classic and FIMO Soft. Also books, videos, tools, metallic powders and a list of classes taught by Maureen Carlson.

General Supplies

Kitchen Collectibles
8901 J Street, Suite 2
Omaha, NE 68127-2436
(888) 593-2436
E-mail: info@kitchengifts.com
www.kitchengifts.com
A source for over 1,200 copper cookie cutters; also makes custom cookie cutters

Memories Kept
26 Perry Rd.
Richford, NY 13835
(607) 657-8392
3-D memory frames

National Artcraft
7996 Darrow Rd.
Twinsburg, OH 44087
(888) 937-2723
E-mail: nationalartcraft@worldnet.att.com
www.nationalartcraft.com
Snow globes, clock movements, music movements, doll-making supplies, ceramic supplies, craft supplies, display stands and electric supplies.

Sweet Celebrations
P.O. Box 39426
Edina, MN 55439-6722
(800) 328-6722
E-mail: sweetcel@maidofscandinavia.com
www.sweetc.com
Source for cookie cutters and other baking tools that work great with clay.

WDP Studio
1757 Killarney Drive
Holt, MI 48842
(517) 699-7788
E-mail: wdpstudio@dellnet.com
http://wdpstudio.safeshopper.com
Carries holeless beads, polymer clay tools, glitter, mica powder and flakes, Artistic Wire and many inclusions for polymer clay.

index

Don't miss these other polymer clay project books!

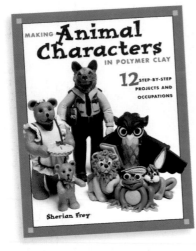

Make colorful and imaginative animal characters! You'll shape everything from rabbits and bears to kangaroos and more—each one with a personality and humor all its own. Includes 14 "animal-at-work" step-by-step projects.

1-58180-041-X, paperback, 128 pages

Polymer clay expert Maureen Carlson provides you with friendly, basic guidance for making the challenge of sculpting likenesses of "real people" both easy and enjoyable. Includes all the techniques you need!

0-89134-927-8, paperback, 128 pages

Create delightful, exquisitely detailed animal sculptures in polymer clay! Inside you'll find step-by-step instructions for 10 charming projects, including a sweet little bluebird, a white-tailed fawn and more! You'll even model animals to look like bronze or jade.

0-89134-955-3, paperback, 128 pages

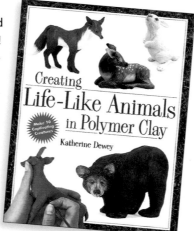

With a little imagination, you'll learn how to bring a whole world of cheery characters to life! Full-color step-by-step photos show you how to make every detail just right, from hair to facial expressions to feet. 21 great projects in all!

0-89134-721-6, paperback, 128 pages

All the techniques you need to create hundreds of polymer clay projects, including buttons, beads, jewelry, figurines, boxes, mosaics and frames! Learn how to create marbling effects, simulate textures, create faux stones and more. It's all here!

1-58180-008-8, paperback, 128 pages